M000004029

Literature Reviews Made Easy

A Quick Guide to Success

Literature Reviews Made Easy

A Quick Guide to Success

Paula Dawidowicz
Walden University

INFORMATION AGE PUBLISHING, INC.
Charlotte, NC • www.infoagepub.com

Library of Congress Cataloging-in-Publication Data

Dawidowicz, Paula.
  Literature reviews made easy : a quick guide to success / Paula
Dawidowicz.
      p. cm.
  Includes bibliographical references.
  ISBN 978-1-61735-191-4 (pbk.) – ISBN 978-1-61735-192-1 (hardcover) –
ISBN 978-1-61735-193-8 (e-book)
  1. Book reviewing–Study and teaching. I. Title.
  PN98.B7D37 2010
  028.1071–dc22

                                                    2010041403

Copyright © 2010 Information Age Publishing Inc.

All rights reserved. No part of this publication may be reproduced, stored in a
retrieval system, or transmitted, in any form or by any means, electronic, mechanical,
photocopying, microfilming, recording or otherwise, without written permission
from the publisher.

Printed in the United States of America

Contents

Preface

T oday, everyone is inundated with information at every turn. The news is shared in newspapers, books, ebooks, blogs, radio, and on television news shows, commentary shows, satirical shows, and even cartoons. How do we know what is useful in making decisions and what is not? How do we dissect what we read or hear to determine how it affects us and, even, whether it should affect us?

I started my analytical career as a high school debater. The concepts of objectivity and inclusion of as many aspects of a topic when conducting an analysis were critical to success, which I experienced. And, with that experience, a world of possibilities opened. It was a world that required a great deal of research, organization, and labor. It was not an easy world, but it was fulfilling, challenging, and exciting. It has taken me on a path through working at three research centers, preparing numerous grant and program proposals, and conducting research for businesses, the military, the government, and in numerous school settings.

My dissertation proved to be one of the most noticeable experiences I had on this journey. Computer programs were less sophisticated, and my familiarity with the existing programs was limited. As you can imagine, my lack of technological ability affected nature of my literature review activities. I had reams of article copies, clipped pieces of paper, and 3 × 5 cards located everywhere as I analyzed, compared, contrasted, evaluated, synthesized, and integrated information I used in my literature review. Working on a topic about which there was little direct research, I mined as many as

Literature Reviews Made Easy, pages xi–xii
Copyright © 2010 by Information Age Publishing
All rights of reproduction in any form reserved.

I could and discovered, evaluating all of it for its usefulness to my research. Picture an 8 × 10 room with papers spread over every surface—desk, chair, and every inch of floor. That was my dissertation literature review process.

The process was more comprehensive than any research I'd ever done. I needed a system to plan, process, and analyze all the material. Thus began the development of the contents of this book—a development that evolved as I tutored students on the development of their own literature reviews and, later, developed a course on writing literature reviews for doctoral students.

The techniques and organization developed through years of experience and the development and oversight of hundreds of literature reviews are shared in this book. Information on how to structure an unbiased review—one that lets you reach beyond preconceived notions or one-sided arguments to discover what's really known and really happening—is placed at the beginning. Following that is a discussion of the methods of examining the literature you find—its value to your topic—that includes both checklists on how to analyze the articles and how to present them. Filled with not only checklists, but tables, charts, and examples, it provides a nuts-and-bolts how-to of the literature review development process not available in other sources.

This book also includes a number of practice and discussion activities, as well as other resources. Its usefulness, as a result, extends to classrooms, whether high school, university, or professional development classrooms. By introducing or encouraging unbiased research, and by providing the tools to make the research process easier, research can go farther faster with greater focus and better results. This book is designed to help do just that.

1

Introduction

This book is designed to help you achieve one specific goal. It's not designed to give you the philosophies of conducting research. It's not designed to give you a background in a specific academic discipline or a specific topic. It's not designed to give you theory. It's designed specifically to instruct you in the practicalities of the writing process used to create strong, thorough, and potentially bulletproof literature reviews.

It fills a gap for people who learn visually, people who want to see the steps that begin with planning the literature review to support a business proposal, grant proposal, dissertation, or academic work and end with a final written product. Although this book won't cover thoroughly the style in which a literature review might need to be presented (APA, Chicago, ASA, AMA, or a specific business or government style), it covers what goes into that review. It guides you through the logic process you need to apply and provides you with examples of writing to help you develop the writing savvy required. It provides lists of questions to help you develop and apply the analysis used in academic reviews, and it includes written examples of

Literature Reviews Made Easy, pages 1–3
Copyright © 2010 by Information Age Publishing
All rights of reproduction in any form reserved.   **1**

how those analyses would read. It also covers information on the types of literature acceptable in academic and in applied professional reviews.

This book is the culmination of years of research experience. It's also the culmination of several years of teaching writing and critical thinking to doctoral students. Although it began as a tool for doctoral students, it has been expanded to be useful for everyone from senior high school students through doctoral candidates working on developing their first literature review or a larger literature review than they normally develop. It has been created for everyone from academics to new business entrepreneurs with good ideas who are trying to write their first reviews to support the new idea they're proposing.

Why Develop a Literature Review?

A literature review is a systematic examination of knowledge available on a topic. In the case of an academic literature review, which is outlined here, it involves the use of appropriate peer-reviewed articles. The reasons are discussed within the main part of this book, but they include the fact that peer-reviewed articles are sources that are designed to be unbiased and objective and to use sources that themselves should be as unbiased and objective as possible.

However, whether you're writing an academic review or a business review, the importance of using unbiased and objective sources cannot be overstated. The use of objective information means any insight you gain into your topic from a literature review is going to be accurate instead of affected by someone's perspective, personal interests, or agenda. The self-imposed measure of accuracy you create by using such objective sources allows you to base the development of your research plan, project, or business proposal on reality rather than speculation. It's hard to create change or discover truth if your basic understanding or beginning premise is faulty. It's also hard to sell a business or a grant proposal, or to maintain support for that business or grant, if you build your plans on faulty information which, inevitably, will be discovered. A literature review written using objective sources and objective information lets you start at that point of strength and knowledge.

Throughout this book, you'll find writing examples. As you use this book, you can also read dissertations and articles in your local universities or colleges or, normally, order materials from colleges and universities through your local public library.

In almost every section there are practice activities. In addition are discussion or writing activities. These are activities designed to let you apply the knowledge shared within the section. If this text is used for a class, any of these activities can be used as assignments or as class or independent discussion topics.

In many early sections additional sources you can use to gain additional information are provided. These sources, as mentioned previously, are available online. In addition, there are numerous lists of questions, sets of guidelines, and several forms provided to help you organize your materials. Many people writing literature reviews today use their computer's database or word processing software to organize their source materials. However, many also still write summaries of each important source, such as an outline, on 3 × 5 index cards. Either way, the forms and checklists provided will help with organizing your thoughts to help you flesh out your literature review.

This book is organized to mirror as closely as possible your literature review planning, research, and writing process. You can use this book in several ways. You can read it cover to cover and use it to get an overall view of the literature review process. You can read each section and use the practice exercises to progressively hone your skills. You can read each section and complete the steps of your literature review covered in that section. Or, you can use it to gather information on specific activities involved in developing your literature review as needed.

2

The Literature Review Process

A literature review is an examination of scholarly information and research-based information on a specific topic. In other words, it's a review of what's *known*, not suspected or assumed, about a specific subject. Its goal is to create a complete, accurate representation of the knowledge and research-based theory available on a topic.

An integral part of a research process, then, is gaining an understanding of what is and isn't known about the reality of a situation, event, or circumstance. One simple explanation for the need to work toward that understanding is this: If people don't know reality, then how can they develop a research study or a plan to address a problem or concern with any effectiveness? An understanding of reality is essential to avoid creating a plan that addresses fiction rather than reality. So, researchers, regardless of academic level or professional position, use appropriate quality literature to accomplish their goals. Although this aspect of a literature review will be discussed in greater depth later in this book, its importance to the integrity of a literature review is so great that it becomes part of the basic definition.

Literature Reviews Made Easy, pages 5–17
Copyright © 2010 by Information Age Publishing
All rights of reproduction in any form reserved.

5

Before proceeding much farther, though, it's useful to reconsider the nature and purpose of a literature review for a moment. By using the current body of knowledge to develop a literature review, a researcher can extend the information making up that body of knowledge and, in turn, extend the understanding of the topic being researched. In other words, when a literature review is followed by original research like that done in a dissertation, doctoral study, or thesis, the body of knowledge (or amount of knowledge) on that topic can actually be increased. That increase in knowledge allows people to both plan more appropriately as they design programs and also design further research that, in turn, adds even more to the body of knowledge on the topic they're examining.

In other words, knowledge of current research and literature versus knowledge of potentially biased or inaccurate information in the popular press can allow practitioners to develop programs and research that can create change. By the same token, theories and actions developed based on information acquired through popular press sources may, if accurate at all, tell researchers only one thing—what the people who wrote that material were thinking about the topic. Bias and objectivity will also be considered later.

Types of Literature Reviews

Literature reviews can be done at all levels of education. They're also often used in business, government, and nonprofit environments as part of individuals' and organizations' planning processes. Needless to say, each of these literature reviews can be distinctly different. These different types of literature reviews can be broken into three basic categories: simple, applied, and academic.

Essentially, a simple literature review is done to gain a brief overview of a topic. The quality of sources is important, but it is not essential that the sources be purely academic. Often such simple reviews are a short compilation of ideas, so popular sources can prove appropriate and useful. However, even in a simple review, popular sources versus academic sources are identified as such so that their value can be judged accordingly.

Applied literature reviews are used in business, in government, and in other professional environments where fact finding is important to a decision making or planning process. Often such reviews involve practical considerations like marketability and profitability figures. Such reviews still have much in common with the literature reviews being discussed here. They almost always include a section on the nature of the change being considered. They require objectivity, and they require accuracy. They will examine the relative value and relevance of different information sources, as well as the latest insights surrounding the results of similar programs or actions. In fact, the most successful proposals have substantive reviews of literature and relevant material on their topic and, as a result, follow the same principles provided in this book.

Academic literature reviews are the review type discussed most often in this book although, as stated here, all three types of reviews benefit from the principles and methods presented in the chapters that follow this one. Academic reviews are designed as either stand-alone products for classes or as precursors to conducting some type of study or project based on current research-based best practices. They require a number of qualities to be of value: accuracy, quality resources, objectivity, thoroughness, and strong analysis. They also require attention to detail, good organization, and a depth of knowledge other reviews may not.

The differences between each of these categories will be described in the following discussions on selecting and narrowing a topic, selecting literature sources, and identifying goals. However, as you read the remainder of this book, remember that, whether a literature review is for an office project, a high school class, or a dissertation, the same principles will apply to each in order to maximize success.

Selecting a Topic

The process of developing a literature review begins with selecting the right topic. Regardless of the level of education for which the review is being written or the professional environment in which it will be used, the topic should be one that will sustain interest for the length of time it will take to complete the extensive research required to finish the project. In the case of a simple review, that time period might only be a few weeks. In the case of a dissertation, the time frame could be much longer—sometimes up to two years.

In all cases, developing a literature review will involve developing a question or questions. What is it that needs to be answered? What is the curiosity or the purpose? These answers will help frame the question or questions and will help determine the content of a successful literature review, so they're very important.

If it's an academic review, the research question should be designed to fill a gap in information available in literature about a topic. In other words, it should provide people with information peer-reviewed research hasn't already provided. It should address a research need. The literature review's goal, then, will be to determine what is known, what is still needed, and how a specific study being considered can help fill that need.

If it's an applied review, it will to survey known information about a topic and help identify information that is not yet known so that best decisions for action or for further examination of a situation can be made. In other words, filling a gap in the literature isn't the main goal. The main goal is an understanding of existing and missing knowledge. The question or questions used should guide that kind of applied knowledge acquisition.

If it's a simple review, the question will normally be more general, as will the survey of the literature conducted. The question will be one that dictates an overview of the information provided in numerous sources on the topic being considered. It will also be one that lays the groundwork for future research of greater depth. In other words, it will provide insight into areas that will each be reviewable in greater depth in future research.

Consider Your Time Period

How long can a literature review take to develop? If it's a literature review for a secondary school or undergraduate class (a simple review), it might take from a month to three months. If it's a literature review to support a grant proposal, a project development plan, or a case study of a program (for an applied review), a literature review development process might take no more than a month or might take as much as a year. The time constraints will be determined by the depth of research required and the broadness of the topic at hand. For example, literature reviews required to support some government grant proposals can be as much as 200 pages, which will take a considerably longer time than the 20-page reviews required for other projects. Senior projects, Master's theses, or doctoral dissertations can take up to a year.

Consider How to Narrow the Topic

Narrow the topic until the question or hypothesis is specific enough for a comprehensive literature review to be completed. Managing to narrow a topic is often one of the biggest problems researchers face, regardless of educational level or professional environment. As humans, people often want to address the big problem—how to cure low income student failure, how to increase productivity in a company with several productivity-related issues to consider, or similar complex questions—which is simply too large to be answered in a reasonable period of time and in a reasonably sized document. There are simply too many pieces of knowledge that must be known and, among them, too many pieces of knowledge that are missing for the information to be acquired and written about thoroughly and effectively enough. If that were not the case, all children would be doing well in school and all companies would be succeeding,

Narrowing Your Topic

First, people benefit from drafting several questions to get a feel for how different questions can address different aspects of the topic being considered. Then, people can examine those questions to see whether they need answers to subquestions that are part of answering the larger question. If there are important subquestions, either plan on including those questions in your research or narrow your topic to explore only one of those subquestions.

Keep in mind that if your question has subquestions you may not be able to answer the large question until you've conducted a study on the smaller question. Why? Your subquestion may have its own subquestions. Let me give you an example.

You're interested in studying why female adolescents in urban areas don't major in mathematics and science in college as often as males. Your question is:

What factors make female adolescents in urban areas less likely to enter mathematics and science higher education programs?

Your subquestions could be:

- What cultural factors, if any, make female adolescents in urban areas less likely to enter mathematics and science higher education programs?
- What educational factors, if any, make female adolescents in urban areas less likely to enter mathematics and science higher education programs?

If we make a small change to your major question, you'll find some subquestions need to be answered before the major question can be addressed effectively. Here's an example: What factors make females less likely to enter mathematics and science higher education programs?

One subquestion might be:

- What cultural factors, if any, make female adolescents less likely to enter mathematics and science higher education programs?

However, with that subquestion, you need to break your literature review questions into smaller subquestions, like:

- What familial factors, if any. . . .
- What community-related factors, if any . . .
- What cultural factors, if any . . .

Identifying Subquestions

If you're not limiting your research to a specific location or even a certain research population in a specific location, your topic may be too big for you to meet the requirements to research it thoroughly enough to create a solid literature review or solid study. The fact is questions that are too large—that involve too many factors, too large a population, or too large a geographic area—require you to have so much background knowledge of your topic to draw valid, supportable research-based conclusions that you may never be able to finish your literature review, your research study, or your business proposal. Limiting questions, populations, environments, or topics can be essential for your success.

If you're doing a literature review for a case study or an applied project, or if you're doing a simple literature review, you won't need to be as detailed in your analysis. In the first case, you've already greatly limited your populations' potential variable characteristics. In the second place, you're not expected to draw the type of detailed conclusions as are necessary for an academic literature review.

Small Research Questions and Larger Research Questions Have a Distinct Relationship

Normally, the small questions are answered by research studies over a period of time, all of which incorporate a literature review to help people gain an understanding of the realities of their topic. In the social sciences, the large questions normally can't be answered before those years of subquestion research occur. Once those smaller studies occur, the new information generated is combined to create a new, higher level of understanding.

If you want additional help with the question planning process, examine the brainstorming and organization sections of this book. Using those methods can help you identify topics and factors to consider as potential question and subquestion areas.

Further Narrowing Your Topic

Having discussed questions and subquestions, and how they define your literature review, it may seem ironic to now add the idea of narrowing your topic. However, one characteristic of a literature review that the consideration of questions and subquestions illustrates is that it's not just a matter of identifying all of the factors and characteristics of your sample population that you need to consider as you create a review. You need to create realistic limits to the topic you study. Otherwise, you'll never be able to do a thorough enough literature review to gain a solid understanding of your topic and its variables.

Regardless of the type of literature review you prepare, you will not have to read every article on your subject. For both applied and academic reviews, though, you will have to read enough to get a thorough picture of the body of research and the spectrum of perspectives that are available. To accomplish this without making your literature review your life's purpose (or the equivalent in time required to complete it effectively), you may have to narrow your topic.

Narrowing your topic becomes even more imperative in part because, with too broad a topic, your efforts in research collection can encompass so many topics and so much information that you can lose focus. As a result, a literature review that is already unwieldy can quickly become totally overwhelming. As you narrow your topic, consider the following:

1. Who will be interested in your question? Why is it important to them?
2. What period of time do you need to consider in your review? For some discussions, a history of the work on the topic is important. For others, only recent knowledge and activities are important.
3. What type of literature does your review topic require? This question is the focus of the next section.

Remember, as you consider how to narrow your topic, that a literature review is different from a research report. Often research reports focus on literature that supports your perspective. However, a review of the literature should cover work that supports not just your initial perspective, but also enough other perspectives to create an unbiased understanding of your topic. Again, for assistance with narrowing your topic, you can review the brainstorming and organization sections of this book.

So, as you consider who will be interested in your question, why it's important, how much time it will take to consider it, and what types of literature you will use, remember you're not considering just one perspective. You're considering multiple perspectives to draw objective conclusions.

Selecting Literature Sources

What types of literature are useful in a literature review? In any review of literature, you'll use research-based articles. You'll also read locally written articles relevant to your topic and situation or event. As mentioned earlier, you do not have to read every article available on your topic to complete a comprehensive review. In addition, depending on the project involved, it can be preferable if you're doing a simple literature review or an applied literature review to do a more focused review of literature so that your information doesn't become unwieldy.

Local Sources Versus Research-Based Sources

That said, the process of identifying your literature review sources can be a long one. Depending on your topic and the type of review you're do- ing, you'll want to use some quality research-based sources and you'll want to include some sources that are local to the situation or event you're ex- amining. For most applied literature reviews and for all academic literature reviews, research-based sources will be peer-reviewed journals.

What ratio of these two types of sources—local and peer-reviewed—will you want to use? That depends on your literature review and purpose. For simple literature reviews, an equal mix of local and research-based sources is normally appropriate. For an applied literature review that is part of an on-site case study, you will normally need more local sources than research- based sources. However, your ratio will be dictated by your topic and goals. If the literature review is part of a grant application or similar product, the significant bulk of sources used will be research-based sources. Finally, for an academic literature review, local sources will be used only as part of your evaluation process, which is discussed later in this book.

How many sources do you need for your literature review? There is no numerical answer for that question. The answer is that you need enough sources to let you gain a solid, unbiased picture of your topic. You'll want to have several sources that draw the same conclusions about a topic, but after that you'll want to begin search for other perspectives and conclusions about your topic. Remember, the goal is to create an unbiased discussion of aspects of your topic. More details on how to do that are covered in the section on brainstorming in this book.

Research-Based Sources

In academic literature reviews, the majority of articles will be drawn from peer-reviewed and refereed journals. Such articles are printed in journals because the journals' reviewers have determined that the information shared in them is valuable and meets rigorous research and analysis standards. The reviews of the articles are done by reviewers who do not know who wrote the papers, so the decision to publish a given article is based on the work done rather than the name of the author. This helps guarantee that the information presented in such journals is strong and has integrity.

Books versus Peer-Reviewed Articles

As you search for research-based sources, you may come across numerous books you feel are appropriate for your literature review. They're written by a professor at Harvard or Yale, or perhaps by a world-renowned expert on your topic. They contain enlightening information.

Should you use those sources? There is no simple answer, since those sources may have value. The authors will have documentable background in your topic. However, there are a couple of other considerations. First, everyone has some type of bias, regardless of how much people work to control it. Even experts in a field may not see a situation as clearly as they might. Second, there is no blind peer review of the information shared in books.

A blind review of an article is a review of that article by several (normally three) researchers in the field who are not given the author's name. Instead, the article and the study it describes are judged on their own merit. The reviewers separately examine the basic framework (basic perspective or philosophy) of the article developed as a result of the literature review (similar to yours) that the author conducted and partially presented in the article itself. Was that framework developed as a result of an unbiased examination of previous research?

Reviewers also consider whether the research procedures and analysis met academic standards—large enough participant samples, appropriate samples, appropriate data sources or participant questions, and appropriate meticulous analysis. They also consider whether the conclusions drawn appear appropriate based on the data acquired. Were the conclusions logical? Were they appropriately limited or generalized to the group examined?

Only if an article meets required academic standards is it published, which is very different from the publication of a book. You can see the rigor to which peer-reviewed articles are subjected. You can understand, also, why books are not considered as valuable, when developing a literature review, as peer-reviewed articles.

Selecting Research-Based Sources

So, how do you find the research-based sources you use? Often, when you conduct a search of peer-reviewed articles, you'll find you either have a large volume of articles from which to choose or you have almost none. Since there are few topics that are totally unresearched, if you find you have few sources, you might want to consider trying new search terms. If you find you have too many sources, you might want to consider adding some additional search parameters that will limit your large number of articles a little more.

Once you have a group of peer-reviewed articles from which to choose, you'll need to narrow the number. A good first step is to review the articles' abstracts to discover the type of research done, perspectives used and, potentially, the results of the research. Since your goal is to read material on as many different perspectives, and presenting as much new information as possible that's relevant to your topic, abstracts give you an opportunity to flesh out a planned reading list. Remember, you will have already narrowed your topic so you can successfully develop your literature review. Be careful not to veer from that narrowed topic.

Selecting Local Sources

Since local sources can be biased and, potentially, manipulative, they have a limited value in most literature reviews. However, they can help people understand the human dynamic—how people feel about a topic or situation, how people feel about other people, or how people react to a certain event. These sources can also provide details of events that may not be available otherwise.

Here are some examples of situation-specific or event-specific sources:

1. newspaper articles that give details, statistics, and other facts related to your topic and your particular situation or event.
2. newspaper articles that share people's opinions about your topic or about the event or situation you're examining.
3. journals of individuals who experience the situation or event you're examining.
4. historical accounts of the topic, situation, or event you're examining.
5. video recordings or broadcasts on a topic, situation, or event.

Although some of these sources have a specific use—providing statistics, numbers, participants, and more—about your situation, they're not always appropriate to use. At times, those facts can be trusted, and at times they can't. You as the researcher must be a discerning user. Whenever possible, check your facts with several sources.

Local sources that describe people's feelings or that quote people do not provide objective information. However, by providing people's opinions and emotions, they tell you how people are responding to a situation. This knowledge is important in *academic literature reviews*, but is particularly important in *applied* and *simple literature reviews*. It is something that must be considered when evaluating an environment for which you are either developing or evaluating a plan of action, or developing a research study. So, these articles have value as long as they are not confused with objective research.

When developing an *academic literature review* or, in most cases, a project to address a need, though, you will find yourself relying more on academic research sources. These sources will most often be peer-reviewed articles that provide a detailed review of the topic you're examining. You'll use articles in various peer-reviewed journals and other materials that you can apply to your specific environment or situation. More information about peer-reviewed sources is provided in a following chapter on the nature and quality of sources available for your use.

In addition, a discussion of tailoring a literature review to the specifics of the situation you are considering occurs later in the book. Here, I will focus on peer-reviewed sources to foster your ability to both conduct and present high quality analytical literature reviews and will only touch minimally on the use of other sources.

Peer-Reviewed Articles

Peer-reviewed articles fall into several categories. They include reviews of relevant literature created by others, literature summaries (reports on articles, not analyses), study reports, policy discussions, and examinations of quantitative and qualitative methodologies. Each type of study has a specific purpose and value to dissertations, depending on the topic.

However, just because a piece of literature is a study report does not mean it's a study report appropriate for a literature review. It needs to be the report of a study published in a peer-reviewed journal. Each of these types of literature is reviewed in some detail here and in greater detail later.

A literature summary does just what its title says it will do. It summarizes a number of articles on a topic. The summary is not of the articles as a whole. It includes a summary of only those portions that are related to the topic being studied. As part of this summary, the articles and information are examined for relative value and validity.

A study report is similar, although it focuses on a study that has been conducted. It covers every step from framework through conclusions, presenting the information in a comprehensive manner. The presentation includes a discussion of the various perspectives considered in the process of developing the framework upon which the study was based.

A policy discussion analyzes rationale for a policy or the effects of a policy. The analysis is done using peer-reviewed journals. Such policy discussions are valid because of their attempts at objectivity. If at any point the material presented is not as objective as possible, the author can lose credibility.

Identifying Goals

To summarize, the goal of a literature review is to gather the most current information from the body of knowledge on a given topic you are researching. Some of that information will be contradictory and will present different perspectives. In your literature review, you will present the information, consider its value, and draw conclusions based on that presentation and consideration.

Practice

1. You're curious about the concept of nature versus nurture and what that means to students in middle school. Who might be interested in that topic, and how could you narrow it? What peer-reviewed journals could you use?
2. Your business has just implemented a new Information Technology program. You're curious about how this will impact frontline customer service representatives. Who would be interested in your question? What peer-reviewed sources could you use?
3. The nonprofit agency where you work has a teen pregnancy program. You're interested in the potential impact of the program on the teen mothers' decisions to get Master's degrees. Who would be interested in your question? What peer-reviewed sources could you use?

4. You've always wondered whether it made a difference in people's days if they exercised at the beginning of the day or at the end. Who would be interested in this information, and what peer-reviewed sources could you use?

5. Spending time in the sun is your favorite activity. You wonder what emotional difference it makes for teenagers who get exposed to sun for at least 5 hours a day. Who would be interested in this information, and what peer-reviewed sources could you use?

Discussion or Writing Activity

Choose a topic of interest to you for your literature review. Consider the following:

- Who would be interested in it.
- What sources you could use.
- Whether it is narrow enough.
- What your ultimate use of it will be.
- Any concerns you have about the use of that topic and how to develop your literature review.

Answering this information within your text, create a 1–2 page discussion of your topic.

Other Resources

http://www.utoronto.ca/writing/litrev.html
http://library.ucsc.edu/ref/howto/literaturereview.html
http://www.library.cqu.edu.au/tutorials/litreviewpages/what.htm
http://www.library.cqu.edu.au/tutorials/litreviewpages/why.htm
http://www.library.unsw.edu.au/~psl/itet_lilt/lit_review/litrev1.htm

3

Objective Research

Literature reviews provide overviews or histories of topics. They present the logical development of theories or ideas. Researchers accomplish this based on their examination of data and research already presented by others. They include reports on studies. These reports include summaries of the theoretical and research frameworks used to design the studies, as well as the studies' methodology, data gathered, and results. They include articles on policies—analyses of backgrounds, analyses of results, and analyses of people's attitudes. Finally, they include examinations of quantitative and qualitative methodologies that have been used in the studies discussed in the articles being examined. All this is accomplished using a specific format and requiring specific content.

Where can you begin in developing such a literature review? Literature reviews conducted by others, if current and objective, can give you a place to begin your own literature review research. They can also give you an example of how a literature review should look and how it should read. However, what if the literature review isn't objective? How can you tell?

Literature Reviews Made Easy, pages 19–22
Copyright © 2010 by Information Age Publishing
All rights of reproduction in any form reserved.

Identifying high quality literature review writing is something you'll learn as you read and study this book. However, objectivity is something you must understand to begin creating a quality research product now, at the beginning of your research process. It is, therefore, considered here.

An objective researcher considers a number of parameters of (or factors involved in) a given circumstance. Those parameters help explain the circumstance's characteristics, evolution, maintenance, conflict with other circumstances, devolution, or other conditions. Peer-reviewed articles on those parameters show what other researchers have concluded about their relative impact. They show which factors, or parameters, other researchers have considered and which they haven't. They show what conclusions other researchers have drawn based on their research, and they provide you with the knowledge to evaluate the quality of those conclusions. For an *academic literature review*, they will be the cornerstone of developing objectivity. For *simple* and *applied literature reviews* where peer-reviewed sources are not used, the same requirement for objectivity exists. So, if you are working on one of those types of literature reviews, evaluate your articles and sources for objectivity and bias using the same requirements as those of an *academic literature review* writer.

To perform objective research, you as a researcher need to use a structured process.

1. You identify your topic and narrow it sufficiently.
2. You identify some initial parameters of, or factors impacting, the topic you're going to examine. For example, if you're examining the impact of changes in male-female interaction in small businesses resulting from the increasing number of female-owned businesses, you might examine these factors:
   a. Male–female communication styles.
   b. Communication styles of different ethnicities and races.
   c. Communication styles in small versus large businesses.
3. You begin searching articles on your topic.
4. You create an outline of the points you will consider under each parameter after you've read enough of those articles to give you a preliminary idea of both the research that's been done on your topic and the results of that research.
5. With your outline in hand, you research articles that explore the pros and cons, confirmations and denials, and modifications of the results of those initial articles and their results.
   a. This step is important, because it allows you to create an unbiased work.

b. Part of your research will be an analysis, comparison and contrast, evaluation, synthesis, and integration of the articles you research.

c. Your end result will be the core information for a discussion of your topic relating directly to your question and the particular circumstances you're examining.

Practice

1. You work in an office for a small, woman-owned business where you've noticed that women are not in positions of leadership. It sparks in you a curiosity about whether this is a common occurrence in women owned businesses. What question might you use?

2. You're studying special education, and you're particularly interested in the experiences of special needs middle school students in inclusive environments when they have Attention Deficit Disorder. What might your question and subquestions be?

3. You're a psychologist with 20 years experience working with parents of Sudden Infant Death Syndrome (SIDS) babies. You've observed some patterns in their behavior, and you want to conduct a study on the long-range impact of SIDS on parent's self-esteem.

4. Your job requires you to travel randomly from time zone to time zone. You live in Illinois in the Central zone, but have made 3 trips to California, 2 trips to Florida, 5 trips to Colorado, and 1 trip to Alberta, Canada in the last month. You notice that you're beginning to have trouble sleeping on a regular schedule. You're having trouble thinking, and you're experiencing random body pains. You wonder whether the mild depression you're noticing is related to the Circadian rhythm shift you're experiencing or whether it's because of the stressful job you have. Who would be interested in your research, and what peer-reviewed sources could you use?

5. You love aquariums, and notice that they help you relax. You wonder if there is a difference in people's responses to larger versus smaller fishes. Who would be interested in your research, and what peer-reviewed sources could you use?

Discussion or Writing Activities

1. When conducting research to decide what information with value exists on a topic and how that information can be used to further knowledge or action in an area, researchers shift from

writing summary reports to writing literature reviews composed of research analyses and arguments.

To prepare:

- Consider the differences in the process and content between a summary and a literature review.
- Think about how objectivity fits into this discussion of summaries vs. literature reviews.
- Consider the challenges you think might arise when developing a literature review research argument that wouldn't arise when developing a summary report.

Either discuss in class or write a 2–3 page discussion on this information. Use examples to illustrate your points.

2. Identifying objectivity can be difficult. To prepare, consider arguments you've found presented in the news, in articles, in books, and in your work environment. Ponder the following questions:

- Which of those arguments were presented objectively, and which were presented in a biased manner?
- What differences were there in the topics of those arguments? Do you see a pattern in the types of topics that are presented objectively or with bias?
- What differences were there in the types of sources used to support those arguments? Do you see a pattern in the types of sources that are used to present objective arguments and the types of sources that are used to present biased arguments?
- Were the objective arguments presented effectively, or did they appear to be biased even when their creators stated they were meant to be objective? What specifically made them effective, or what made them ineffective? Do you see patterns in the arguments that made them effective or ineffective?

Either discuss in class or write a 2–3 page detailed discussion of the difference between objectivity and bias and the importance of using objectivity in a literature review. Use examples to illustrate your points.

Other Resources

http://www.utoronto.ca/writing/unbias.html
http://www.englishbiz.co.uk/popups/objectivity.htm
http://lgxserver.uniba.it/lei/foldop/foldoc.cgi?objective+-+subjective

4

Generalizability and Transferability

Consider this fictitious example: someone works in a small rural hospital in Northern Maine. As the head nurse there and a graduate student, the person decides to conduct a study on the impact of overtime caused by inclement weather on the small staff and the resulting tension with the doctors.

Why is the small study important? It's just a little hospital in a little place, and all of the people are individuals who may not respond in the same way as the people anywhere else, right? What difference do the findings make to "the big picture?"

The example presented above is just one potential situation where researchers can ask the question: Why is that research important to anyone but the individual doing the study or the small organization being studied? The answer is important to understand when considering any literature review design, or even any potential research question.

Unlike pure scientific studies that identify universal causes and effects (i.e., x causes y and without x there can be no y), social science studies deal with humans who are variable by their very nature. Rarely can exact causes

Literature Reviews Made Easy, pages 23–26
Copyright © 2010 by Information Age Publishing
All rights of reproduction in any form reserved.

and effects for actions be identified. Instead, social scientists often have to accept being able to establish only the fact that two things may occur at the same time rather than causing one another (*a correlational relationship*).

Given that information, the question of the value of various studies is important. How relevant to nursing in other locations is what is found in the small hospital in rural Maine? At the same time, is there value in studying a small business in Toledo, OH to a person living in Los Angeles? Is there value in examining a volunteer training program for a small local health center in Albuquerque, New Mexico for someone running a national hospital chain?

For social scientists, the goal is normally not to conduct research for the sake of pure knowledge acquisition. As a result, most social science researchers find themselves forced to answer the question: So what? Why is this research important? Why is it not a gathering of random information that will sit in an obscure article in a seldom-read journal in a stuffy, cramped library on the extension campus for a minor state university?

Researchers find the answer to that question in two words: *generalizability* and *transferability*. Each is considered here.

In his consideration of qualitative research, Myers (2000) explained that generalizability is a relationship determined by the nature of the study population and the larger population. In other words, if the pertinent characteristics of the small nursing population are similar enough to the pertinent characteristics of the nursing population in other small hospitals, other rural hospitals, or even to other hospitals in total, then you have a condition where findings can be generalized to the appropriate larger population.

Notice that, when Myers (2000) speaks, he does not mean that something generalizable must apply to all of humanity. For example, generalization of the hospital study could mean the generalizability of study results to all rural hospitals, all rural hospitals with certain types of nursing demographics, all rural hospitals with certain types of specializations, or all rural hospitals clustered around some other factor not identified immediately here. Similarly, in other types of studies, generalizability could refer to groups like all women of a certain age; all firefighters; all 3rd grade students; or all rural high school students in the Northeast, Southwest, or in total.

Myers (2000) suggests that much social science research is not generalizable. It can, however, be considered as a starting point when examining similar groups, and it can help provide more in-depth insights on a topic that will allow researchers to consider in greater detail similarities and differences between research environments and another environment of interest to you or readers of your review.

Here are some examples of generalizability.

1. The ability to predict that all mainstream 3rd graders experience an explosion in vocabulary growth in modern mainstream educational curricula.
2. The ability to predict that #% of nurses will quit within the first year.
3. The ability to predict that children will at some point experience separation anxiety from their parents.

Note here that the common words are *the ability to predict.* That means that if something is generalizable people can predict with a measure of certainty what will happen in the group to which research findings are generalized.

Transferability goes hand in hand with generalizability. The decision to transfer research and conclusions from one environment to another is made by readers. Readers may observe any of the following:

1. A similarity in circumstances.
2. A similarity in groups.
3. A potential total or partial explanation for an occurrence or phenomenon.

What does this mean? There may not be enough research done on a specific group (say 3rd graders) to be sure the majority of them, or all of them, will have a given experience. However, there may be research that indicates that the experience has occurred among a number of 3rd graders in urban environments.

This means you will want to consider the circumstances and results of this related research as you consider what to research about the group you're going to study. Will your sample have the same experience? You should consider this topic as it relates to your literature review topic and groups. For example, what about rural 3rd graders? Will they have the same experience?

Considering whether that information can be transferred to rural 3rd graders also gives you somewhere to start when you consider your research questions. Other ways to consider that information are to examine whether it can be transferred to other similar groups of students (perhaps 2nd graders or suburban 3rd graders).

Hunting for transferability is sometimes called *mining the data.* Mining the data means looking at a circumstance that's similar and considering whether what you know about that circumstance can be applied to your situation. In other words, will the information you know about one situation apply to another, similar situation? Since it can be a valuable research and literature review technique, this approach will be discussed more in following chapters.

Practice

Consider your potential topics. Based on this information, can you design your question to allow generalizability or transferability of information? Write a few versions of questions that would allow generalizability or transferability. Further, as you do your brainstorming, outlining, and assessment of articles, make sure you keep generalizability and transferability in mind.

Discussion or Writing Activity

Select one of your topics. Consider the following:

- Your ultimate goal for your literature review.
- The characteristics of the specific group you're going to study or develop a project to impact.
- Who the information in your literature review can be generalized or transferable to and how it might be useful to those other groups.

Draft a 1–2 page paper explaining your plans. If you still haven't decided on a topic, consider drafting a description of several of your topics. Describing on paper what you plan to do can help you determine which of these topics might work best for you.

Other Resources

http://writing.colostate.edu/guides/research/gentrans/com2b1.cfm

Reference

Myers, M. (2000).Qualitative Research and the Generalizability Question: Standing Firm with Proteus. *The Qualitative Report, 4.* Retrieved from http://www.nova.edu/ssss/QR/QR4–3/myers.html.

5

Quoting and Paraphrasing

Before considering brainstorming and organization, where you'll find yourself recording some information you read, understanding paraphrasing proves helpful.

Paraphrasing is integral to academic success for several reasons. The first reason is connected with the use of quotations, the other method of sharing information provided by other authors.

Quotations within literature reviews detract from the writers' demonstrations of ownership of the knowledge shared in the literature they've read. If literature review writers don't understand information and its importance well enough to rephrase that information in their own words, it's questionable to readers whether the reviewer will be able to effectively analyze it.

In addition, quotations tend to include information that is irrelevant to the specific topic being examining. That extra information acts as *noise*, distracting readers from fully appreciating or, sometimes, even understanding the points the writer is using the quotation to help create or support.

Literature Reviews Made Easy, pages 27–33
Copyright © 2010 by Information Age Publishing
All rights of reproduction in any form reserved.   **27**

In addition, to maintain the structure of the quotation and let the information make sense, sentences incorporating quotations often must be structured differently. The result is that those sentences can be more awkward and, as a result, harder for their readers to process. Not only does the extra information create noise, then, but the change in sentence structure required to *make sense* of the quotation being used affects the flow of the paragraphs and of the arguments being written.

In other words, the rewording required to use quotations can cause readers to struggle with trying to process awkward argument construction. The use of paraphrasing, instead, can help readers seamlessly understand and remember the point.

As previously stated, readers can interpret the use of quotations to mean that writers don't understand information enough to accurately rephrase that information. That is, perhaps, the biggest problem with using quotations. If writers aren't able to explain in their own words what someone else is saying, then readers can lose faith in writers' ability to process and apply it to their own topic.

Generally, quotations should only be used when the wording used by an author is so exact and so valuable that a writer can't rephrase it better. Otherwise, writers' should paraphrase the information they share from other sources. So, when reading something, ask yourself whether the words used by the author are the only, or the best, way to express what the author is saying. Then ask yourself whether any extra information is included that isn't necessary. If the answer to the first question is no or the response to the second question is yes, then the quotation isn't perfect as written by the author and should be rewritten by you.

How you cite a quotation is based on the writing standard you're supposed to use. Since most social scientists are required to use APA formatting for their professional writing and for journal papers (*academic literature reviews*), APA formatting is used as an illustration here. However, in either a *simple* or *applied literature review*, any number of styles could be used. Such styles could include Strunk, MLA, or even Chicago style. The style used will depend upon the consumer of the literature review. If it's a *simple review* for a class, it would likely be done using the Strunk or MLA style. If it is an *applied literature review*, it could use the format of the publication for which it's written (like Chicago) or could still use one of the more formal, academic styles. To make your decision about style, consult with your consumer about expectations.

This book uses APA style because, again, that is the standard for academic social scientists. Using that style, when creating a quotation, you place quotation marks at the beginning and end of the material you quote. Then, you put an appropriate citation in parentheses just outside the closing quotation before putting a period at the end of the sentence. It would look like this: "The price of tea in China is directly related to the amount of tea that makes it to market" (Smith, 2004, p. 25).

Please note that the name of the author, the date of the publication, and the page number are included in the citation. This particular quotation and its source are fictitious, but they do provide an illustration of the standards for citing a quotation. However, giving you additional information in this book on how APA citations would look for all of the various types of resources you might use would force the creation of a second volume. So, please consult the *APA Manual* (2011), referenced formally in the *Other Resources* section, for exact citation information.

Writing can be difficult enough without being unsure about whether you've used the information you gather from your sources correctly. Although one method of using the information in whatever essay you're writing is *quoting*, it has just become obvious that using quotations is not always necessary or desirable. So, *paraphrasing* is another alternative for using the information you gather effectively and correctly.

A paraphrase *does not use* the words used by the author whose information is important for your own work. A paraphrase, instead, is a rephrasing of the information you've read. Perhaps the best way to understand what this means is by considering some examples.

Read the following information. It is created to illustrate proper paraphrasing.

> Numerous reasons were identified for high school students electing to attend college. Numbers of both rural and urban high school students indicated they were bored with their environments and saw college attendance as a chance to experience new challenges (Jeffries, 2001; Davis, 2004; Jermaine, 2005). In addition, urban low income students saw college as an opportunity to escape poverty (Kauffman, 2006). High income high school students indicated a third motivation—the desire to please their parents (Crane, 2005).

To paraphrase, first read the material and consider it in the context of the topic you're researching. That will determine what pieces of the material you're reading will be important for you to paraphrase.

Let's say your topic is whether students' reasons for acquiring higher educations impact their success. You will find different information important for that topic than if your topic is whether students' economic status during early education impacts their success in higher education settings. If your topic were a third area—whether students have clear expectations of the role of higher education in their futures—you could even find other information important.

So, your first step in this example was to read your material, keeping your topic in mind. Your topic was whether students' reasons for acquiring higher education impact their success.

As you read, it struck you as important that both urban and rural students applied for college because they were bored and saw college as a chance to grow.

You wondered whether that perception would affect their outcomes. The results could either support or contradict the concept that economic status impacts students' educational success. You want to share this information. How do you paraphrase it?

1. There are no exact words that are *the* right answer. There are, however, some words that will make a paraphrase *not* an acceptable paraphrase. Here are some examples of how to avoid creating those *incorrect* paraphrases.

2. If you reread the text several times, make sure you reread it *after* you paraphrase to make sure you haven't accidentally used the words you read. Using the author's words would make it *incorrect*.

3. Do not use pieces of the text inside your paraphrase. Remember, you cannot use part of a sentence in your paraphrase and have it be acceptable. One exception might be if there's a word or two used as a name for a specific event, circumstance, or occurrence. That word can be used without quotations *unless* it is a term coined by the author you've read which would require quoting.

(a) Example 1 from the information above.

Jamison stated that such researchers as Jeffries, Davis, and Jermaine determined that *both rural and urban high school students* felt *bored with their environments* and believed that going to college was *a chance to experience new challenges.*

(b) Example 2 from the information above.

Numerous researchers determined that, whether rural or urban, many students believed college would be *a chance to experience new challenges* (Jamison, 2006, p. 23).

Note that both of these incorporate some of the wording. How many words used from the original source are enough to make paraphrasing incorrect? Here's an example of what would be allowable:

> Numerous researchers determined that, regardless of whether they're rural or urban, notable numbers of students believed that college was an opportunity to *experience new challenges* (Jamison, 2006, p. 23).

One exception to this rule would be the use of a proper name. If a proper name, such as the name for a law, a school, or something similar is used in the article you read and is made up of several words, it can be used in your writing without being in quotations or needing to be cited. *However, remember that if you learn something about such an entity or program in someone else's writing, you'll want to cite the author as your information source for the paraphrase.*

4. You cannot read a paraphrase by your author of another author's work and cite the original author instead of the author you personally read. You cite the author *you* read. Otherwise, your paraphrase is *incorrect.*

Example from the information above.

Numerous researchers determined that, regardless of whether they're rural or urban, notable numbers of students believed that college was an opportunity to *experience new challenges* (Jeffries, 2001; Davis, 2004; Jermaine, 2005).

You cannot change the meaning of the text. If you're focusing on a different topic from the author, you can share only those pieces of the article that are important to your topic. However, you cannot *add to, delete from,* or *misrepresent* the information the author presents.

(a) Example 1 from the information above.

Numerous researchers determined that, regardless of whether they're rural or urban, students believed that college was an opportunity to experience new challenges (Jamison, 2006, p. 23).

(b) Example 2 from the information above.

Numerous researchers determined that, regardless of whether they're rural or urban, notable numbers of students believed that college was their chance to have greater challenges than their parents had (Jamison, 2006, p. 23).

As you can see, these manipulations can be slight. However, they all make your paraphrase *incorrect*. What are those changes? In example (a), *notable numbers of students* has been changed to *students*. The difference is in the implied number of students who demonstrate this belief. In example (b), the paraphrase includes an inference that the original author meant people wanted to experience more challenges than their parents had. Instead, the original stated only that they wanted to experience new challenges without stating what they expected those challenges to mean or to be.

Finally, here's one example of a way this information could be paraphrased well:

Among the reasons researchers have identified that numbers of students, whether urban or rural, apply for college is that it will provide them with new challenges to experience (Jamison, 2006, p. 23).

Note that part of what makes this paraphrase correct is the citation of author, date, and paragraph or page number.

Reference (fictitious example)

Jamison, J. (2006). Why students attend college. *T H E University Journal, 30*(10).

_____

Practice

Examine one article you want to use in your literature review. Identify some information shared by the author you wish to share. Following the steps above, paraphrase that information.

Discussion or Writing Activities

1. Do an online search of articles from the *New York Times*, the *Washington Post*, or a newspaper local to you. Read 5 articles in their entirety. Practice paraphrasing the important points in each article. Make each paraphrase only one paragraph long so that you're forced to select only the most important points.
2. Visit the other resources listed below, and connect to the paraphrasing links they suggest. Several paraphrasing exercises and quizzes are offered at different university websites. Use the exercises. Then take the quizzes, and see how you do.

Other Resources

http://www.waldenu.edu/c/Files/DocsWritingCenter/writing_the_lit.ppt
http://www.waldenu.edu/c/Students/CurrentStudents_3670.htm
http://www.utoronto.ca/ucwriting/paraphrase.html
American Psychological Association (2011). *Publication manual of the American Psychological Association.* (6th ed.) Washington, DC: American Psychological Association.

6

Selecting Quality Sources for Your Review

It's important to understand what sources are acceptable for a quality review. It's also important to understand that the nature of quality sources can change if you're producing a simple, applied, or academic literature review.

Small Reviews of Literature

When developing literature reviews, you set out to familiarize yourself with the existing body of knowledge on your topic. Therefore, the sources have to reflect high quality research. Why? High quality, logic-guided, bias-free research allows you to get as close as possible to the reality of a circumstance and, to create positive long-term change, people need to understand reality. So, examining literature that provides quality, science-based insights provides the basis for developing a quality circumstance-based plan to create change.

What articles qualify as quality articles? That can be an easy question to answer, or it can be a hard question depending on the type of literature review you're creating.

Literature Reviews Made Easy, pages 35–40
Copyright © 2010 by Information Age Publishing
All rights of reproduction in any form reserved.

_____

Academic Literature Reviews

For academic literature reviews, quality articles are considered articles published in peer-reviewed journals. Peer-reviewed journals judge articles submitted to them based on the quality of the research conducted and the conclusions drawn by the researchers rather than the general reputation of the authors. Basically, journal staff members send three reviewers a blind copy of the article (a copy without the author's name on it). The reviewers read the article and, if it meets the journal's standards and is accurate, well-researched, and has sound conclusions, recommend it for publication. Such a judgment based only on the text and not the name of the author ensures an objective evaluation of the article and, as a result, the sharing of quality information in the journal.

If you have access to a number of good-quality peer-reviewed articles, how do you decide which are most valuable? It depends in part on where you are in the research process. If you haven't decided yet which factors about your topic you're going to research, you can examine them all to identify what factors about the topic have been researched and what that research tells you about the topic. To do this, you can conduct a good database search and review the abstracts of applicable articles. That search can help you with brainstorming and with developing your preliminary outline. It can also help you identify some initial sources to read and consider.

If you've decided which dimensions of your topic you're going to consider in your literature review (what factors you'll examine), you can look for articles about those dimensions. Say the topic is the effectiveness of community volunteers in teaching HIV prevention to high school students. You've decided to explore two specific dimensions—students' attitudes about instruction from volunteers versus paid health or education providers, and the age or sex of the person providing the instruction. There might be three articles on the topic. A summary of them follows.

- High school-aged students respond better to individuals who are contemporaries rather than people who are the age of their parents.
- Volunteers prefer working with students who are attentive rather than students who are in cliques and talk throughout the presentation.
- High school-aged students attend informational sessions outside the school environment less often than they do within the school environment.

Consider the relative value of these three articles.

1. The first article is directly related to the topic because it answers who students might accept most as instructors.
2. The second article is also related because it indicates that volunteers may treat students differently. This could affect whether or not students respond better to volunteers than to paid professionals. The questions connecting these articles to the topic would be whether paid professionals respond to students in the same way and whether volunteers' feelings are identifiable by students.
3. The third article is not easily connected to the topic and questions being considered. To use it, you would have to assume students would respond well to meeting with volunteers better if they met inside school. However, that doesn't really contribute to your understanding of the questions you've identified.

You will find many articles that you can justify as being somewhat or slightly related to your topic, if you wish. However, examining those articles will make your literature review less focused and effective. The result can be a loosely related review with points that are not made well, if made at all. It will be a review that demonstrates no ability to create strong, coherent research and that is longer without being better.

How can you use those peripherally related articles? One common method researchers use is to create a file for them so the articles can be used at a later date or in other research, perhaps follow-on research. That way, the focus of the literature review stays intact but the articles are kept for possible use later.

So, look for articles that relate directly to your topic and the factors you're considering. Remember, though, to think outside the box, so that you can gather as much applicable information as possible. This process of examining data about related or similar topics (child discipline and adolescent discipline, corporate subdivision management and small business management, post-traumatic stress disorder anxieties and social anxiety) is called *mining the data.* It can prove particularly useful if there is limited data or are limited articles on your topic.

Related to the HIV instruction question, if *mining the data,* you may find information on students attending career counseling instruction from volunteers that will give you some insight into student participation. It might also give you some insight into how students respond to volunteers and, perhaps, whether the specific age and sex of the people conducting counseling is important. So, you can gather information that is directly related to your questions but that doesn't necessarily appear to relate to your topic from the viewpoint of the average reader.

Finally, remember not to create too speculative a web of ideas as you examine the literature. As you gather information that fits outside the box, make sure it does actually relate to your topic directly in some manner. Straining the relationship too greatly by trying to create connections that may not actually exist can corrupt your research process and make your literature review ineffective.

Timeliness of Articles

One last consideration is the timeliness of the articles used. The goal of a literature review is usually to examine *current* literature to understand the current state of the body of research-based knowledge on a topic. How much information is available on your topic, what's considered current by the people to whom you're accountable for your review, and how much groundwork you need to lay with older sources to create a framework for whatever current information is available are decisions that need to be made on a case-by-case basis, often with input from any fellow researcher collaborators or by a dissertation committee.

Sometimes, there is no current literature on a topic. It may be cutting edge, or it may be something that appears to be overworked years since. In such cases, older information is often a main focus in a literature review. Thinking outside the box to gather important, appropriate information on the topic is often also a large focus of such a review.

Applied Literature Reviews

If you're developing an applied literature review, you can never go wrong using peer-reviewed resources similar to those discussed above. However, you may not find an extensive number of peer-reviewed sources on your topic. Perhaps your topic involves legal precedents, statutes, or laws. Perhaps it involves government or military reports.

At some point, it needs to be related to current research or thinking on the topic. If you cannot find many peer-reviewed articles on your topic, you can use articles on similar topics, discussed earlier in connection with *academic literature reviews* as *mining the data*. In addition, you can look at historical peer-reviewed sources on your topic or a related topic.

If there proves to be little peer-reviewed information on your topic, there is yet another possibility. As part of any person's review on a topic, some local sources will be used. These sources are not peer-reviewed. Instead, they are sources like newspaper articles, magazine commentaries, and unrefereed journal and book sources. If nothing else is available, these sources can be used. However, because your work is professional, as much as possible you will want to *mine your data* for other sources that can help explain the topic, circumstance, event, or occurrence you're examining.

Remember, your goal is to be objective in your gathering and presentation of data, so you want to gather as much peer-reviewed data, or local data, so that you will have the optimal opportunity to be unbiased and objective in your presentation and conclusions. Remember to weigh peer-reviewed literature more heavily in your examination of literature sources because it is designed to more rigorously meet objectivity standards.

Simple Literature Review

Again, as in an applied literature review, you can never go wrong with peer-reviewed sources. However, your topic may be so expansive and your treatment designed to be so exploratory that you might choose to look only at popular literature on your topic. If that is the case, your sources would be newspaper articles, magazine articles, bulletins and reports published by interested individuals, and other common sources.

The caveat with using these sources as the bulk of your literature review rather than as additional sources is that you need to develop as objective a review of the literature as possible. That is much easier to do with peer-reviewed articles, so if you are instead creating a simple literature review drawing on popular sources you must take particular care to develop it.

Practice

Using three questions of your choice, review various abstracts for academic online databases or academic library-based articles that discuss your topic. Remember, you may not have narrowed your focus completely here. Your goal is to see what peer-reviewed articles are available on your topics. What topics have been considered and what haven't surrounding your topic. Take notes on what has and has not been researched, as well as what is directly related to your topic and what is more loosely related to your topic.

Discussion or Writing Activity

Since you're beginning to look at quality resources for your topic, it's a good time to begin recording information in those articles for later use in your literature review. So, although your topic may not be completely defined, it will prove useful to begin using the forms supplied in the Appendix of this book.

1. Make copies of the Article Analysis Form and the Critical Thinking Chart.
2. Read articles for your literature review research, and take notes on those articles in the Critical Thinking Chart.
3. At this point, as you read abstracts for peer-reviewed articles you believe may be useful to you, you can make a list of the factors considered in research about your topic.

Although you will not use these forms as they were designed to be used, using them as you start your research can help you keep your data organized and in one central location. This is an activity you should continue each time you read an article because it may help you organize and structure the literature review.

Other Resources

http://www.languages.ait.ac.th/EL21LIT.HTM#what
http://www.lib.utexas.edu/lsl/help/modules/peer.html
http://www.lib.calpoly.edu/research/guides/peer.html
http://www.hsl.creighton.edu/HSL/Guides/Lit-Review.html
http://info.wlu.edu/literature_review/library.html

7

Brainstorming: Examples of Factors to Consider

$\mathbf{I}$n this chapter, the focus is on the mechanics of preparing to develop an outline for your literature review. Before you can develop that outline, you need to do some brainstorming.

Two popular methods for brainstorming are free writing and clustering. Examples of them follow. Although some people prefer to go straight to creating an outline as they plan their literature reviews, using these methods can help ensure a more full, complete understanding of what to research and include in your literature review even during the initial stages. This can maximize the effectiveness of your work.

Do you need to consider all dimensions of, or all factors involved in, your literature review topic? No, you don't. Here's an illustration.

You're examining the impact of democratic classrooms on teacher morale. Here are a number of factors involved in democratic classrooms and teachers.

Literature Reviews Made Easy, pages 41–49
Copyright © 2010 by Information Age Publishing
All rights of reproduction in any form reserved.   **41**

1. Size of the classroom—large, small, medium.
2. Number of students—0–5, 6–10, 11–15, 16–20, 20–25, 25–30.
3. Openness of dialogue—always, sometimes, never.
4. Responses of teachers—open, closed, mixed.
5. Responses of students—active, grudging, none, animated.
6. Respect shown by students—sometimes, grudging, always, never.
7. Homework completed—never, sometimes, always, detailed, minor.
8. Amount of work that can be accomplished in a class—varying by schedule, number students, etc.
9. Subject being taught—open to discussion, not open to discussion, physically oriented, academically oriented.
10. Age of the students—preschool, elementary, middle, secondary, adult.
11. Age of the teacher—early 20s, 30s, 40s.
12. Years of teaching experience—0–2, 3–5, 6–10, 11–20, and 21–30.
13. Background of teachers—urban, rural, strong family, weak family, good student experience, poor student experience.
14. Background of students—strong family, weak family, good supervision, weak supervision, physically active, not physically active, healthy, unhealthy.
15. Home life of teachers—good, bad, stressful, money problems, relaxing.
16. Home life of students—encourage school, don't encourage school, lots of activities, not many activities, lots of supervision, not much supervision, talk to parents, not talk to parents.
17. Courses being taken by students—large load, small load, difficult, simple, academic, physical.
18. Number of courses being taught by teacher—small load, moderate load, large load, overload.
19. Whether there are democratic classrooms and undemocratic classrooms in school—examples from other classrooms, no examples, stress between teachers and in classrooms because of differences in treatment, etc.
20. What impacts teacher morale—fulfillment, ease of work, excited students, etc.

Examining this list, it's obvious there are many different possible circumstances to consider when examining the impact of democratic classrooms on teacher morale. How many of these are important to examine when considering the impact of democratic classrooms on teacher morale? How many should you consider? Should you consider them all?

The reality is that you could never finish your work if you considered every variable unless you wanted to spend years preparing to write the literature review. Even then, you'd barely get everything done only to have to start researching new literature on the same topics, because as research is being evaluated new literature is being published. So, what do you examine?

What variables are most important to your specific situation, your specific area of interest, or your specific circumstance? If you're interested in an urban setting, then perhaps you don't need to worry about rural information. If you're interested in at-risk youth, do you need to consider students who are happy, have strong home lives, and are doing well in school? They provide a good contrast with students who experience the opposite. However, *if* your articles on at-risk youth contain comparisons and contrasts surrounding at-risk and well-adjusted youths, *you don't need to review materials on "well-adjusted" youth, do you?*

How many factors should you choose? There is no solid, specific answer to that question. It will be dictated in part by the type of literature review you're developing—simple, applied, or academic. It will also be partially dictated by the amount of literature available on your subject.

If you used the practice activity in the previous section of this book, you've gotten at least a sense of what's been researched on your topic. That can help you consider what you wish to research as you consider which variables, or factors, are most valuable in your examination of your topic. However, narrowing your focus and being specific about your interests and goals is very important to your success.

Brainstorming

As you consider what dimensions of your literature review topic you're going to examine, try both free writing and clustering forms of brainstorming. Sometimes, a two-step planning process—free writing and then clustering the ideas generated in free writing—can help people decide both what to include in the outline and where to include it. As you work through this book, take the opportunity to see what works best for you.

Free Writing

To illustrate this, here's an example of using free writing. The topic in which you're interested is the potential usefulness of adapting a management training program used by Fortune 500 companies for teachers. The question could be: What impact would the use of a Fortune 500 management training program have for training teachers? Here are your free writing steps:

1. With plenty of paper in hand, find a quiet place to consider the question.
2. Set aside a specific amount of time to consider the question with a minimum of 3 minutes and a maximum of 20 minutes reasonable. (There will be time in there when your mind wanders, so you may need to get a feel for the length of time that is optimal for you. You also need to do this at a time when your mental distractions will be minimal.)
3. Write down every thought that occurs to you in relation to this question, whether it seems initially important or not. Your thoughts don't have to be written in complete sentences as long as you will understand when you review them later.

Your results might look like this:

1. Teachers' students are like unmotivated employees.
2. Managers, teachers need to instill self-motivation, self-monitoring.
3. Depends on age of child—young maybe, older yes.
4. Difference in measures of success teachers/managers need to be considered.
5. Does type of work environment matter to management training program/students?

As you can see, the ideas jotted down aren't all following one logic path. They aren't even complete sentences, unless having complete sentences becomes important to understanding them later. The benefit of this open brainstorming that doesn't follow a specific logic path is that it leaves you free to identify the many directions you may need to go. Remember, this is a preliminary activity, so this exploration of many directions is essential to identifying the any and all directions you need to pursue in your literature review.

In addition, each of those directions, or factor development paths, can be pursued using free-written after this initial free writing activity is completed for a deeper examination of them and their importance to your topic. However, you don't want to create too many layers of this free writing activity because this is still part of your consideration and speculation stage.

The ideas jotted down in free writing activities can be used to develop clusters using the clustering activity that follows. If you choose to bypass the clustering process, they can become the factors used to develop your outline, if you've gotten enough ideas to flesh out your literature review. If you have few factors identified for inclusion in your outline, the clustering method is probably a necessity for sorting those ideas and developing more ideas.

Clustering

Clustering is another brainstorming technique. As you read the comments on free writing, it may become obvious why clustering is useful after using free writing. Free writing can help you generate a lot of ideas, and clustering can help you sort those ideas and extend the areas you wish to analyze.

As with free writing, you will have to identify which of these planning methods, or both, is useful in planning your work. For clustering, once again, you use the same materials.

1. With plenty of paper in hand, find a quiet place to consider the question.
2. Set aside a specific amount of time to consider the question with a minimum of 3 minutes and a maximum of 20 minutes reasonable. (There will be time in there when your mind might wander, so you will need to get a feel for the length of time that is optimal for you. You will also need to do this at a time when your mental distractions will be minimal.)
3. Write down every thought that fits into clustering in relation to this question, whether it seems initially important or not. It helps to express thoughts in short, self-designed abbreviations, as long as they can be understood later.

For this activity, you:

1. Draw a circle in the center of your paper.
2. Write a couple of words inside the circle that act as an abbreviation of your main question.
3. Draw a short line out from your circle and, at the end, jot a specific idea you have. Each of your thoughts will be extended out of your circle using a different line. Eventually, your circle will appear to have a series of spokes extending from it, similar to the spokes extending from the center of a bicycle wheel.
4. After identifying those spoke points on the circle of your central identified question, draw lines out from those points to iden-

tify the next layer of analysis you can consider about your main question—the analysis of your *spoke* points.

This process can continue—with more and more layers of analysis being formed—for as long as continuing to expand the cluster to develop the literature review proves helpful. For a small literature review, the depth will be much shallower than they would be for a dissertation.

Or, as mentioned earlier in the book, if you need to dig into your topic to a level where there is a research gap or so that your topic is small, narrow, and very specific, you can continue this process until you've identified a small enough, narrow enough topic that you can look at it clearly and thoroughly. In other words, you can continue this process until your topic and subtopics are narrow enough to become workable for you in terms of time and of the potential scope of your study or proposal.

For the following example, the question is: What impact would the use of a Fortune 500 management training program have for training teachers? For the purposes of spacing, this will use the abbreviation *teachers/managers*. A basic clustering of the topic is shown in Figure 7.1.

As an additional example, the cluster in Figure 7.2 considers criteria to examine when evaluating literature on voters' reactions to a presidency.

Again, if you're building on the free writing activity, you can use this chance to cluster the ideas you developed in your free writing activity to take your analysis to deeper levels than initially identified in free writing. That activity is demonstrated in this illustration. If you're better at using free writing or even going straight to an outline, then you might skip these brainstorming steps. However, you might give these both a try during the activities following this lesson so you can decide which you prefer.

Once you've got a clear idea of the factors and variables involved in the topic you're considering, you can return to *The Literature Review Process* to consider the questions you've asked. As you complete your planning, remember to narrow your topic so that it's manageable and relevant to your overall question or questions.

Note: If you use these two planning activities in sequence, you will benefit from taking a time break between these two activities. That break will give you a chance to return to your ideas with fresh thoughts. You might find yourself expanding your initial list of ideas and, as a result, creating a better quality plan for your literature review.

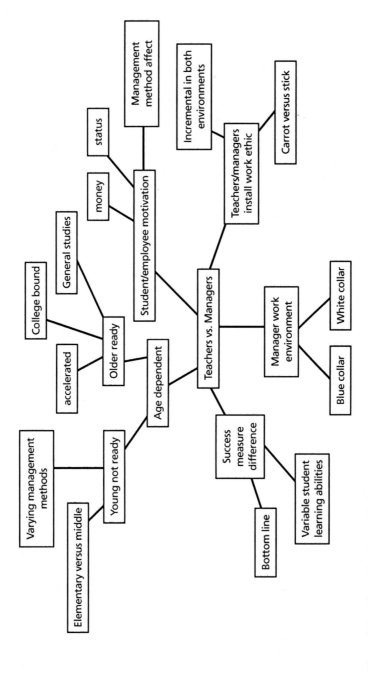

Figure 7.1 Clustering Example 1.

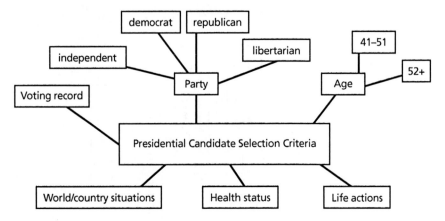

Figure 7.2   Clustering Example 2.

Practice

Take three questions of your choice, and narrow them as much as possible. Use free writing with one question, clustering with the other, and both with the third. See which one is more comfortable for you.

Writing Assignment

The goal of this book is to help you learn to develop a literature review. To develop your literature review, you'll use articles in various databases and from the libraries you use.

In this writing assignment, you will declare the topic you've selected to examine in your literature review. Write a 250–400-word description of the literature review you propose to develop. Be sure your description includes/addresses the following:

1. What question are you researching?
2. Why did you select this question? That is, what is your reasoning in selecting this question, and why is the question important?
3. Having used the free writing or clustering method to identify them, what factors or variables (the spoke points surrounding your central question if you used clustering) must you consider to create an objective literature review?
4. Since you cannot consider them all in your literature review, select the factors or variables about your question you're going to examine in your literature review. What are they, and why did you select them?

5. Using the clustering method again, what aspects of the topic do you need to consider about those four or five factors you selected in Question 4 if you are going to create an objective examination of them?

6. What sources will you use to begin your literature review?

Be succinct. Specificity and brevity are important when you write a literature review.

Other Resources

http://web.umr.edu/~gdoty/classes/concepts-practices/free writing.html
http://writing2.richmond.edu/writing/wweb/freewrite.html
http://www.humboldt.edu/~tdd2/Freewriting.htm
http://www.sdcoe.k12.ca.us/SCORE/actbank/tcluster.htm
http://www.graphic.org/goindex.html
http://www.unc.edu/depts/wcweb/handouts/literature_review.html
http://www.libraries.psu.edu/instruction/infolit/lst301h/condlitsearchrev.htm

8

Creating an Initial Outline for Your Literature Review

Over the years, a number of writers have said they don't write their novels and stories. Instead, their characters write them as their stories evolve. They, as authors, don't find out who "did it" until they write those last words. If there are authors who really use that organizational style, their style is not the style you will use in planning your literature review!

Before beginning this consideration of the importance of outlines, it's necessary to make an unequivocal statement. *A literature review outline should be a living organism that is given the same consideration as any pet or honored member of the family. For your literature review, it is a family member that needs to be fed, groomed, and given attention often.*

That said, one of the easiest ways to organize a literature review is to use an outline. Most people have seen the classic outline format.

Literature Reviews Made Easy, pages 51–54
Copyright © 2010 by Information Age Publishing
All rights of reproduction in any form reserved.

Getting Ready to Write the Outline

Before beginning to write an outline, you may have read some information about your topic. Your sources might be peer-reviewed or non-peer reviewed depending on your topic, your type of literature review, and their availability. If you have not read much about your topic and find your free writing or clustering charts do not have much detail, consider visiting an academic library or an online academic database and doing a search on articles about your topic. It's hard to create an outline for a topic without any knowledge about that topic, so see what the abstracts of articles tell you was examined related to your topic. That search may give you new ideas to add to your research plan.

What the Outline Looks Like

The outline starts with main headers, which equate to Level 1 headers in APA-style papers. The first subheader equates to a Level 2 headers in APA-style papers. The next level equates to Level 3 headers, and the next, or final level, would equate to paragraph headers.

A Moment About APA Standards

Why is APA format mentioned here? It is the accepted academic writing standard in most social science disciplines, so it is used throughout this book. If you're using Strunk or another standard, please follow the requirements of those resources. The American Sociological Association, for example, does have a different writing standard, but it's very similar to APA standards. You might even be using Chicago style. Regardless of style, however, your outlining as an informal pre-literature review tool can still be organized as it is in the example provided in this chapter.

Back to Your Outline

So, what do you put into your outline? Let's look at an example based on the teacher turned manager idea used previously.

    I. Introduction
        a. Topic question
        b. Why important
    II. A Comparison of Roles
        a. Discussion of nature of teacher
            i. Smith (1925, p. 23)—teacher caregiver

      ii. Jones (2000, p. 25)—"a teacher is perceptive and inter-ceptive"

  b. Discussion of nature of manager

      i. Abercrombie (2003, p. 423)—manager mentors success-ful employees

      ii. Fitch (2004, p. 78)—manager most responsible for busi-ness success

  c. Similarities in roles

      i. Both manage the environment

          1. Jefferson (2004)

      ii. Both are role models

          1. Jackson (2001)

      iii. Both are held accountable for outcomes

          1. Irving (2004)

  d. Differences in roles

      i. Importance of differences in age

          1. adult versus child

             a. Jackson (2001)

             b. Jefferson (2001)

          2. teenager versus child

             a. Brown (2000)

             b. Barton (2006)

      ii. Importance of differences in types of management

          1. factory versus school

             a. Breakman (2006, p. 26)—"the modern school is like a factory"

          2. office versus school

             a. No one yet???

Notice that there are authors listed throughout this outline. If you've conducted an article abstract review, you may have information on which articles you're going to use to discuss your points. If you haven't, then you won't. That's all right.

If, eventually, you still find no research on a given possibility and it still appears relevant to your analysis of your topic, that point is still important to mention. In that case, you state that the point is a consideration that should be researched in the future because the knowledge gained may prove important to a future understanding of your topic.

As illustrated here, the outline also can include some quotations and some ideas that jumped out at you, as articles were reviewed. You can streamline your writing process by jotting down ideas developed during your reading as they occur to you for two reasons. First, you won't forget any ideas that pop up, and you have them placed in your writing so they're easily integrated as you write. Second, you will differentiate quotations from paraphrasing by placing them in quotation marks from the beginning. That use of quotations helps you ensure you won't inadvertently plagiarize which can destroy your credibility and create major problems because it is an ethical violation.

Your outline, or notes about the articles you'll use, may not look the same as the example used here. Perhaps you write sentences instead of using header titles. If you do, those sentences could end up being the topic sentences used in the introductory paragraph of a section of your review, or they could end up being the topic sentences for paragraphs within those sections.

Practice

Choose one of the questions you used for your brainstorming. Review those brainstorming notes, and create an outline. If you need to, visit an academic library or online academic database and review the abstracts of peer-reviewed journal articles on your research topic to gain additional ideas on topics that should be discussed in your literature review.

Discussion or Writing Activity

Produce a 2- to 4-page written synopsis of your outline. Make it as exact and succinct as possible. This written version, in conjunction with your outline, allows you to conceptualize more clearly your literature review as a whole, what it will include, and how it fits into your overall research or project development agenda. Remember, you're creating a living document here. Treat this development as such.

Other Resources

http://www.library.unsw.edu.au/~psl/itet_lilt/lit_review/litrev3.htm
http://www.unc.edu/depts/wcweb/handouts/literature_review.html

9

Types of Article Examination Used in a Literature Review

Regardless of the purpose for, or type of, literature review—simple, applied, or academic—all literature review developers are researchers. As such, they all need to adhere to the strict requirements expected of researchers. Such strict requirements, or rigors, include objectivity, appropriate thoroughness, and the application and written presentation of sound critical thinking methods. This chapter gives a basic overview of the critical thinking methods all researchers apply when developing a literature review.

There are a number of names for the six higher order thinking skills used within literature reviews. They are *analysis* (sometimes called evaluation or examination), *comparison, contrast, synthesis, integration,* and *evaluation.* An examination of Bloom's Taxonomy (Overbaugh & Schultz, n.d.), which is available on hundreds of websites, will illustrate this point. At times, other skills or skill titles are indicated or used. Just search for "Bloom's Taxonomy." However, they can be distilled into the skills discussed here.

Literature Reviews Made Easy, pages 55–60
Copyright © 2010 by Information Age Publishing
All rights of reproduction in any form reserved.
55

Please note that, although there are several names used to refer to each of these skills, it is the term *analysis* that is most often overused. Not only does *analysis* refer to a specific skill, it's also a term people use to refer to the whole group of skills that allow academic examination of a topic. Every attempt has been made to avoid that issue in this book, hopefully successfully. Here *analysis* is one of several skills you need to use to do a quality literature review.

Speaking of different uses of terms, it's important to mention that often comparison and contrast are combined into one analytical method, as are synthesis and integration. They are treated differently here because they look different, act different, and are two relationships that complement each other. If one side isn't clearly understood or well executed, the other side will be ineffective. Though the literature review will be less effective and, potentially, ineffective.

Since the goal of this work is to provide clear understanding of, and examples of, the parts of a literature review, this information organized so that each of these complementary critical thinking methods is treated separately and in some detail. The importance of this decision will become evident in the following chapters and you apply the information provided here to the development of a literature review.

The six skills discussed in this book work together to help people develop a strong assessment of the strengths, weaknesses, and applicability of different resources to the overall understanding of the literature. It also helps you identify the knowledge available about a specific topic. This book pulls each of the skills apart and examines examples of each in future chapters, but here is a brief overview of these skills and how they fit together.

Analysis is the first and most basic consideration of literature that researchers perform. In it, they examine the nature of the article itself. What are its basic assumptions, and are they sound? What is its structure, and does it present information clearly enough to be sure the study and the researchers' conclusions are sound? What evidence does it use? Is it appropriate and accurately used? What reasons for the results does it present? Are they appropriate to the method used, and are they accurate? What conclusions does it draw? Again, are they appropriate to the method used, and are they accurate? What logical implications do its conclusions have? Is there any piece of the information presented, or method presented, that makes you uncomfortable or uncertain about the accuracy of the results and conclusions?

What does that mean? When researchers analyze (review, evaluate, consider, examine) an article, they look at its basic integrity. If it's the summary of a study, you examine such factors as the nature and size of its sample group and the quality of the sample group. You also examine whether any research conducted was done and presented correctly, whether the conclusions drawn were appropriate and accurate based on the methodology used and data gathered, and whether the new information was integrated correctly into the body of knowledge you are creating. If it's a review or summary of literature, you look at the quality of the research used, whether the research used was presented accurately, and whether the conclusions drawn were appropriate for the research examined.

That makes analysis perhaps the most important type of research examination method. Analysis determines whether the article has value in total, has parts of value, or has no value. It also determines whether the article is worth using in other types of analyses.

Comparison and *contrast* go hand in hand, as mentioned earlier, but it's important to conduct comparisons first for reasons that are described later. A comparison is an examination and discovery of patterns of similarity within two or more articles. Similarities can occur in any of the major characteristics of those articles—basic assumptions or frameworks for the studies discussed, structures of the studies, and evidence cited in the studies or cited in the articles being reviewed. Similarities can also occur in the reasons for conducting the studies or for drawing conclusions, in the conclusions themselves, and in the logical implications that flow from the conclusions. More areas of potential similarity will also be discussed later.

As a complement, a *contrast* is an examination and discovery of differences between two or more articles in any of these areas. These two activities—comparison and contrast—when conducted either separately or simultaneously, help people to understand different researchers' specific contributions to the body of literature. This in turn helps people further understand the strengths, weaknesses, and relative importance of different researchers' work.

Evaluation requires using a different perspective to examine the value of specific research and data. It means considering the literature you've examined in your review in relation to the specific topic (event, circumstance, situation, occurrence, program, organization) you are examining.

In any literature review, an *evaluation* proves valuable, but in a dissertation a strong, comprehensive *evaluation* of available data proves essential. Why? An *evaluation* is conducted to consider how strong some evidence, conclusions, and implications are in relation to an outside topic—in this case, your specific topic. That application tests the accuracy of the information being applied. In the case of a dissertation, the research being considered and justified is important because of how it applies to a specific location or a specific circumstance you're going to be researching. It can be essential to justifying your study of the topic and any further action—conclusions, program, grant, or research study—you plan to take. *Evaluation*, then, creates a bridge between the research conducted by others and the research you're conducting.

Synthesis is an important part of creating the framework used as the rationale of a study. It requires identifying sound parts of various articles that are in harmony with each other. For example, assume the following articles by the following people actually exist. *Smith (2001) presents research on managers' expectations of their employees, and Jones (2003) presents research on the impact of managers' styles in times of stress.* Although not saying exactly the same thing, their research and conclusions do not disagree with each other. In fact, blended together they complement each other to create a more complete picture of what occurs in management environments than people could gain from either article separately.

This information can be combined with *Abercrombie's fictitious research on managers' leniency during regular working periods and Fitch's fictitious research on different responses managers can have to employee attitudes.* When combined, each of these articles contributes information that helps people gain a clearer understanding of the management environment and what it can mean to your question.

Integration is the complementary process of *synthesis*, just as *comparison* and *contrast* are complement each other. In *integration*, the *disparities* of various results and conclusions are explained to effectively present a more complete view of the topic. Just as *synthesis* was meshing compatible research about different aspects of a topic, *integration* is meshing apparently incompatible research about different aspects of a topic. Because this can be hard to conceptualize, here's an example.

> Jones (2003) conducted a study indicating that junior mid-level managers facing audits become highly stressed and less tolerant of employee behaviors they might otherwise tolerate. Smith (2004) found the opposite. His research indicated that junior mid-level managers facing audits had enough support from more seasoned managers to avoid being stressed. However, Smith's research indicated that each of the organizations she examined had strong training programs, including active mentoring, something that Jones (2003) did not include in his research. It appears, therefore, that mentoring programs may reduce the stress levels of junior managers when facing stressful circumstances like audits or similar senior-level monitoring.

Together synthesis and evaluation—based on analysis, comparison, contrast, and evaluation—create the framework to understand the research topic and the importance, potential effectiveness, and relevance of any plans or conclusions researchers draw as a result of their literature review. This framework, well developed, can make a literature review effective. Poorly developed, it can make a literature review irrelevant.

This is just a rough idea of what integration looks like. Again, we'll go into more detail in coming sections of the book, including more detailed examples. Notice, though, that it is a process of identifying how apparently contradictory pieces of research may be combined to complement each other.

To assist you in this process, examine Appendix A. It contains a form you can use to chart the information gathered from each article. It also contains a form you can use to evolve comparisons and contrasts, syntheses and integrations, and evaluations from the information you gather.

Practice

Consider your topic. You've created an outline. Can you identify some locations in your outline where you anticipate the comparison and contrast of various articles or points of view might be useful? Will synthesis and integration benefit your review? What can you use to evaluate your topic? Remember, these ideas are preliminary considerations, but they can help you to continually flesh out and re-evaluate your outline and your literature review's content.

Based on your research and the information included in this book, create an outline for yourself on areas you need to consider as you analyze the integrity of the articles you review.

Discussion or Writing Activity

You've created a narrative about your plan for your literature review that is. Revisit that narrative. Consider where in that narrative you're describing analysis, comparison, contrast, evaluation, synthesis, and integration. Revise your narrative to include discipline-appropriate terminology and clear expression of your ideas, where needed. Consider also where you might introduce additional analyses, comparisons, contrasts, evaluations, syntheses, and integrations that will prove useful for examining your topic. Include those new points in both your narrative and your outline.

Other Resources

http://www.utoronto.ca/writing/critrdg.html
http://www.coun.uvic.ca/learn/program/hndouts/bloom.html
http://www.coun.uvic.ca/learn/program/hndouts/bloom.html
http://honolulu.hawaii.edu/intranet/committees/FacDevCom/guidebk/
    teachtip/questype.htm
http://www.ceap.wcu.edu/Houghton/Learner/Think94/NCmarzanoThink
    .html
http://www.ceap.wcu.edu/Houghton/Learner/think/compare.html#Triggers

Reference

Overbaugh, R. C.. & Schultz, L. (n.d.). *Bloom's taxonomy*. Retrieved from http://
    www.odu.edu/educ/roverbau/Bloom/blooms_taxonomy.htm

10

What is an Analysis?

An analysis (or evaluation, or examination, or consideration), as mentioned earlier, is an examination of the *integrity* of an article. Is its foundation solid? Is the study it presents valid? Are its results accurate and appropriate? How much value, if any, can you attribute to its conclusions? A list of questions to consider as you determine an article's integrity follows.

1. Is the logic behind the study sound? (Does it have a solid theoretical framework?)
   a. Are the literature sources upon which the research design is based sound?
   b. Are they interpreted correctly by the author in the process of laying the ground work for the study?
   c. Is the presentation unbiased, or is it skewed because there is not enough consideration of opposing views and different perspectives on the questions being considered?
2. Is the question being examined sufficiently narrowed, and capable of being tested accurately?

Literature Reviews Made Easy, pages 61–64
Copyright © 2010 by Information Age Publishing
All rights of reproduction in any form reserved.

3. Is the research design appropriate for the question being examined?
    a. If it's a question about a causal relationship, is it an experimental quantitative design or another methodology that allows you to infer causation (such as path analysis)?
    b. Is the sample size large enough?
    c. Is it a biased or unbiased sample?
    d. Is it the wrong type of sample?
    e. Is its methodology suited to examining the specific question being considered?
4. If an article is a not a report of research, are quality resources used in the creation of the article that are treated in an unbiased manner?
    a. Are the sources sufficient and rich enough to draw the conclusions made?
    b. If the article is exploratory in nature (designed only to consider possibilities and not draw conclusions), does it consider enough possibilities to be unbiased and effective?
5. Do the data as reported appear to have been appropriately interpreted?
6. Are the conclusions drawn appropriate for the design and the data collected?
    a. Are the conclusions identified as appropriately limited?
    b. Are the conclusions specific and clear?
7. What are the credentials of the contributors?
    a. Is the author trained and experienced in this type of research, or does the author have credentials in the field?
    b. Does the author use quality sources to establish the argument?

Analysis of an article doesn't involve determining whether the article is of basic use to you. If an article doesn't fit your topic, you can rule it out immediately. However, once that has been decided, analysis can tell you whether the article has value to your own research and literature review because of its quality and integrity.

Here's an example of an analysis:

Smith (2004) determined that there is a correlation between teenagers' consumption of higher amounts of coffee and their tendencies toward the demonstration of Attention Deficit Hyperactive Disorder. However, his study participant selection method was neither random nor representative of varied demographics. His group was drawn from students in three classrooms at one inner city high school. In addition, he gathered no additional information about other factors in the lives of students who did and did not drink caffeine, and he did not gather information on other caffeine sources students may have consumed. He did not include any information on the degree of correlation or the reliability and validity of the measure he used. His method of defining a higher amount of caffeine was not included. His data provided little solid research evidence, but it did raise a question that merits further consideration.

Here's a second example of an analysis, this time a positive analysis of the article:

Smith (2004) examined a potential correlation between teenagers' consumption of caffeine and their tendencies toward Attention Deficit Hyperactive Disorder. In a detailed analysis, he considered the numerous sources of caffeine that can be consumed, and developed a Likert-style scale to report levels of caffeine consumption. After conducting a complete correlative analysis, he demonstrated a preliminary positive correlation between these two circumstances. The more caffeine consumed, the more serious the student's ADHD. That is, higher levels of caffeine consumption were correlated with higher levels of ADHD behavior. However, he pointed out that his study sample was not large enough to establish any definitive relationships between the two, and he suggested this matter bears further examination.

Normally, if an article has no integrity or value, it will appear in a literature review only to demonstrate that the possibility, results, or conclusions were considered so they can be eliminated. In other words, they'll appear to indicate your consideration of your topic was as unbiased and objective as possible. Without a discussion of such articles, the literature review could be considered incomplete because a perspective, possible explanation, or mitigating factor will appear to have been ignored. As a result, the inclusion of such an article analysis can be integral to the success of a literature review.

However, some articles have no integrity at all but do suggest a potential correlation or relationship that should be considered to completely understand your topic. That type of article is shown in the first analysis paragraph. In other words, the data collection or sample may have been minimal, but the importance of examining the article's topic fully might be important.

An example might be a study on why people chew gum. One author's research might focus on a possible correlation between gum chewing and slowed heart rate as a result of diminished anxiety. Although the author used a small sample from which no conclusions might be drawn, the fact that one individual mentioned a possibility can be important to pursue at a later time and might mitigate the results you determine in your own study of the relative strengths and weaknesses of gum chewing.

Note that in the samples all of the articles' major shortcomings have generally been listed. If there were some portions that were strong, they would also be mentioned. However, the overall value would be limited to providing some initial information or ideas either to be examined in other work or to be mentioned as a factor or dimension that requires further research.

Other articles present good information and include an acknowledgement of their limitations and value. The analysis of such articles would be explained within the literature review, and might look similar to the second paragraph. Remember, these articles need to be presented objectively, particularly with regard to their value to your literature review.

Practice

Using three of the articles you have identified as relevant to your literature review, create an outline for each of them answering the questions listed in this chapter. Determine whether your articles have integrity.

Discussion or Writing Activity

Draft an analysis of at least three of the articles you've just analyzed. Explain where they have integrity and where they do not. Write it simply and clearly. Be as succinct as possible.

Other Resources

http://www.library.cornell.edu/olinuris/ref/research/skill26.htm.
http://www.waldenu.edu/c/Students/CurrentStudents_7398.htm;
http://www.library.unsw.edu.au/~psl/itet_lilt/lit_review/litrev5A.htm

11

Creating Structure for an Analysis

Normally, although an analysis may present some summary of the article's information, it is in essence a discussion of the article's integrity and an assessment of its major characteristics for use in future critical thinking activities. Here's how an analysis of an article on parental participation in students' school experiences might look.

> Thompson (2003) conducted a study on the participation of third grade students' parents in three different middle income elementary schools, interviewing 30 parents in each school. Based on those interviews, he concluded that parents who received papers suggesting parent participatory activities from teachers at least twice a week were more involved in PTA, in classroom activities, and in working with their children on their homework assignments (p. 23).
>
> However, Thompson (2003) either did not gather demographic information on the individuals he interviewed or did not disclose the information. In addition, he did not state how or where he acquired his randomly selected participants. As a result, there is no information either on the ethnicity,

Literature Reviews Made Easy, pages 65–67
Copyright © 2010 by Information Age Publishing
All rights of reproduction in any form reserved.

sexes, or employment status of the individuals interviewed. Depending on how the group was selected, the conclusions may be skewed.

Note that the first paragraph contains a quick summary of the information presented in the article. Note also that it presents a brief description of only the most important information related to your topic.

In contrast, the next paragraph presents the analysis, again briefly presenting only the most cogent information. It discusses the strengths and weaknesses of the article, the size of the samples used and conclusions drawn in the study. An analysis might also discuss the research cited in the article as part of its own literature review, if that information is important to understanding the article itself as well as any other factors directly related to the article and its integrity and importance to your study.

If this discussion were continued, the next paragraph might discuss the choice of third grade students and question of what age would be optimal for this type of technique. An additional paragraph might discuss what types of materials would bring about the optimal response. The final paragraph might consider whether, even though specifics that would allow complete understanding of the study's implications are missing from the article, using this type of process bears further consideration.

1. To summarize, here's a brief list of what the presentation of an analysis could look like. Remember that which paragraphs (or parts of a paragraph) from this list you include in your analysis will depend on the integrity of certain parts of the article and on your specific interest in the information presented in the article. You do not need to have all of these topics in your analysis to make it effective. Include only the topics that are integral to presenting your logic—that help your reader understand your conclusions about the article. As pointed out earlier, sometimes selective minimalism can help you develop the strongest analytical presentations.
2. Include a brief summary of important characteristics of article.
3. Include analysis of the strengths and weaknesses of the article.
4. Consider the strengths and weaknesses of the design of the study being reported in the article.
5. Consider the importance of the size and composition of the sample in relation to your topic.
6. Describe any of the other important characteristics considered in your article analysis in relation to your actual topic.

So, an analysis doesn't have to be fancy. It doesn't have to contain a lot of details. It does have to be specific and thoughtfully prepared, and it does need to help the reader understand why and how an article is both useful and trustworthy.

What if you don't want to have separate paragraphs for each of the analytical points you want to share about an article? At times, an analysis doesn't have to be placed separately from the other information in your literature review. It can be incorporated into a comparison or contrast of two different articles. Although comparison and contrast have not yet been discussed, here's a brief fictitious example of such an incorporation of an analysis.

> Smith (2005) found that tea from China was more expensive as a result of the Tea Revolution of 2003, while Jones (2006) determined that it was the result of large tariffs imposed by the United States in 2004 to make United States tea growers' pricing more competitive. However, Jones' results were gathered using a small interview sample and few details were given on the selection method Jones used for the people interviewed. Therefore, Jones' information has relatively less impact value in understanding the phenomenon.

As you can see, there are several structural methods you can use to organize and present your findings. These different methods will be discussed in more detail. For now, remember that somewhere paragraphs will have to include the points mentioned above.

Practice

Choose one of the articles you've analyzed for your literature review. Draft an analysis using the pattern outlined above.

Discussion or Writing Activity

Review the article analyses you wrote. Determine whether they follow the format described above. If not, restructure them to make them most effective. All of the information on one article can be presented in one paragraph if there's little to say but, depending on the volume of material that's important to share, may take several paragraphs. Make the adjustments to your writing based on what you now know.

12

What is a Comparison?

A comparison is a part of your research process that allows you to begin your definition of the characteristics of your topic from a research-based perspective. As with every facet of your literature review, the amount of research-based literature used depends on two factors—the type of literature review you're writing and the availability of research-based literature on your topic. However, regardless of the amount of research-based literature available, the goal is to use unbiased literature to determine those characteristics of your topic, situation, or even population that don't change—those characteristics that are in some way or another similar.

A comparison is decidedly different from an analysis. Remember, an analysis examines the integrity of a specific article, while a comparison considers the similarities between two different articles to see whether they support, or reinforce, each other. This is important, because similarities tell you that specific variables, factors, or characteristics about your topic are the same from one example to another. That means that, as you describe your topic, you can reliably report on that dimension or those dimensions

Literature Reviews Made Easy, pages 69–72
Copyright © 2010 by Information Age Publishing
All rights of reproduction in any form reserved.
69

of your topic, what it means or they mean to your topic, and what occurs regarding that dimension or those dimensions in relation to your topic.

Comparisons can consider a number of types of differences:

1. If what is being examined in two articles is a study:
    a. Similarities in theoretical frameworks (logic, research, and rationale behind the position taken and the research question chosen).
    b. Similarities in research limitations.
    c. Similarities in research assumptions.
    d. Similarities in research design.
    e. Similarities in research study samples.
    f. Similarities in research results.
    g. Similarities in research conclusions.
2. If what is being examined in two articles is a survey of literature or consideration of a phenomenon:
    a. Relevant similarities in histories.
    b. Relevant similarities in culture.
    c. Relevant similarities in religion.
    d. Relevant similarities in accepted or valued morals or ethics.
    e. Relevant similarities in conception of success and failure.
    f. Relevant similarities in ages of relevant entities (individuals, organizations, etc.).
    g. Relevant similarities in location (characteristics, etc.).
    h. Relevant similarities in resources or geography that could be relevant.
    i. Relevant similarities in involved power structures.
    j. Relevant similarities in any other area that becomes apparent through your reading.

In other words, the *similarities* can be structural (theoretical frameworks, research design, limitations, environmental, etc.) or substantive (results, conclusions, perceptions, goals, ages of individuals, etc.).

What does a comparison look like? Read below:

Similar to Jones (2006), Smith (2005) examined the reading performance of a group of 2nd grade students in an urban setting to determine the impact of a 90-minute reading block on students' performance. Although Smith examined 1st grade students, both Jones and Smith examined randomly selected classrooms from randomly selected schools, one group using a 90-minute block and one group not using the block. Both found higher student reading performance on required standardized tests in the schools using the specialized block than in those not using the block.

In this paragraph, you saw an easily identifiable comparison, or a point where one piece of research supported the findings shared in another piece of research. Do your comparisons have to look like this? Not necessarily. Consider this second example:

Hand-in-hand with effective teachers are both democratic education and mentoring programs in which teachers, school administrators, and community members foster personal, interpersonal, and environmental respect and cooperation. Both of these programs interject personal responsibility, good role modeling, and preparation for adulthood into the lives of participating youth (Schechtman, 1993; Haensley & Parsons, 1993).

Note that here, rather than going into great detail, the writer presents only the important information that demonstrates the similarity of these programs. That minimalism can be important to the success of your literature review. Often, the reporting of additional, less important information can detract from the main point you want to share in your comparison.

Note also, please, the citation at the end of the paragraph. That citation indicates the two authors whose articles support each other. This citation is crucial to the integrity of your review, so when creating comparison (or any other assessments based on literature you review), make sure your citations are complete and accurate.

Now, returning to your development of comparisons, what will be common to all comparisons?

1. Credit will be given to all the authors whose articles are being compared, whether mentioned in text and cited appropriately or cited appropriately only.
2. Statement of similarities, whether explicit (This says . . . This agrees with . . .) or implicit [Several researchers have indicated . . . (Jones, 2004, p. 23; Smith, 2003, p. 354)] are supported by citations.
3. There is a contextual tie into the overall topic (introduction of topic and summary that points out the importance of the comparison). This contextual tie doesn't have to be immediately following the comparison. It can occur later and tie in several points made, but it does have to occur in a manner that lets readers identify that your comparison was relevant, as well as how it was important to gaining a greater understanding of your topic.

Practice

Select two articles that demonstrate some similarity as identified above. Write a draft of the information presenting and supporting that comparison.

Discussion or Writing Activity

1. Examine several of the articles you plan to use. Consider the important information to note about them as you compare them, and include that information on the Critical Thinking Chart (see the Appendix for information on this form). Then draft your comparison paragraphs as directed in the *Practice* activity if you have not already done so. Place those comparison paragraphs into your evolving literature review.
2. Review the notes you've made in the Critical Thinking Chart on the articles you've read. Identify other comparison points. Develop paragraphs discussing those comparisons, and integrate them into your evolving literature review.

13

Contrast: The Important Other Side of the Coin

Comparisons and contrasts truly are two sides of the same coin. A comparison considers the similarities between two or more articles, and a contrast does the opposite. It considers the differences between two or more articles. This consideration of the two sides of the coin—similarities and differences—lets you determine some of the characteristics—factors, dimensions, and perspectives—of a topic, situation, or event. What it does is let you *paint a picture* of all of the facets of your topic. By seeing similarities, you can identify facets of a topic that can be grouped together and counted on to create specific responses. You can also identify facets of a topic that, because of identified similarities in various articles and studies, have had their characteristics and impacts on the topic, situation, event, occurrence, or circumstance reinforced.

However, sometimes more can be discovered about the factors, dimensions, and perspectives of your topic by seeing the differences in studies and articles about it. By seeing differences, you can tease out variables in charac-

Literature Reviews Made Easy, pages 73–76
Copyright © 2010 by Information Age Publishing
All rights of reproduction in any form reserved.

teristics, circumstances, or timing that can lead to different outcomes. This knowledge gives you a greater ability to explain the characteristics of your topic, situation, or event, because it lets you know what can change if subtle changes occur within it or within its surrounding environment.

Contrasts can consider a number of types of differences:

1. If what is being examined in two or more articles is a study:
   a. Differences in theoretical frameworks (logic, research, and rationale behind the position taken and the research question chosen).
   b. Differences in research limitations.
   c. Differences in research assumptions.
   d. Differences in research design.
   e. Differences in research study samples.
   f. Differences in research results.
   g. Differences in research conclusions.
2. If what is being examined in two articles is a survey of literature or consideration of a phenomenon:
   a. Relevant differences in histories.
   b. Relevant differences in culture.
   c. Relevant differences in religion.
   d. Relevant differences in accepted or valued morals or ethics.
   e. Relevant differences in conception of success and failure.
   f. Relevant differences in ages of relevant entities (individuals, organizations, etc.).
   g. Relevant differences in location (characteristics, etc.).
   h. Relevant differences in resources or geography that could be relevant.
   i. Relevant differences in involved power structures.
   j. Relevant differences in any other area that becomes apparent through your reading.

In other words, the differences can be structural (theoretical frameworks, research design, limitations, environmental, etc.) or substantive (results, conclusions, perceptions, goals, ages of individuals, etc.). Please note that the wording for this information is almost exactly the same as the wording for comparisons!

As you might now guess, your hope as you objectively read your literature is that you find many similarities between entities being studied and few contrasts. So, it is important to examine critically all similarities and differences in the articles as you read. Your goal is to identify articles that help you substantively improve your understanding of your topic.

What does a contrast look like? Read below to see contrasts presented for the same articles examined in the discussion on comparisons.

> Similar to Jones (2006), Smith (2005) examined the reading performance of a group of 2nd grade students in an urban setting to determine the impact of a 90-minute reading block on students' performance. Although Smith examined 1st grade students, both examined randomly selected classrooms from randomly selected schools, one group using a 90-minute block and one group not using the block. Both found higher student reading performance on required standardized tests in the schools using the specialized block than in those not using the block.
>
> However, Evans (2000) and Jeffries (2003) examined the reading performance of 3rd grade students in rural settings that both used and did not use the 90-minute reading block. Evans (2000) found that neither rural nor urban students randomly selected benefited from use of the block. Jeffries (2003) stated his research indicated the opposite. Using state standardized tests, Jeffries determined that randomly selected 3rd grade students in urban environments did benefit from the use of 90-minute reading blocks.

By adding this second paragraph, you can see the introduction of a contrasting idea based on research. Do your comparisons have to look like this? Not necessarily. Consider this second example that is actually a presentation of multiple potential explanations for an occurrence:

> What reasons could account for the difference in results between Evans (2000) and Jeffries (2003)? It could be the use of different curricula (Leonard et al., 2006). It could be the management of time in the block (Owens, James, & Bettner, 2004). It could be the number of students being retained in the 3rd grade classes being studied (Davis & Thomas, 2004). There are a number of other possible reasons, but Evans (2000) and Jeffries (2003) did not provide enough background information on their studies to determine which of these possible explanations were most feasible.

What will be common to any example of a written presentation of a contrast?

1. Credit is given to both of the authors whose articles are being contrasted, whether mentioned in text and cited appropriately or cited appropriately only. Include citations to support a statement of differences, whether explicit (This says... or This contradicts...) or implicit [Researcher A determined... (2004, p. 25), but Researcher B determined, however, ... (2003, p. 354).]

2. Include a contextual tie into the overall topic (introduction of topic and summary that points out the importance of the comparison). This contextual tie doesn't have to be immediately following the contrast. It can occur later and tie in several points made, but it does have to occur in a manner that lets readers identify that your contrast was relevant, as well as how it was important to gaining a greater understanding of your topic.

Practice

Select two articles that demonstrate some difference identified above, preferably about at least one of the articles you used in the previous chapter on the comparison to help reinforce your ability to see both similarities and differences between any two articles. Write a draft of the information presenting and supporting that contrast.

Discussion or Writing Activity

1. Examine several of the articles you plan to use. Consider the important information to note about them as you contrast them, and include that information on the Critical Thinking Chart. Then draft your contrast paragraphs as directed in the *Practice* activity if you have not already done so. Place those contrast paragraphs into your evolving literature review.
2. Review the notes you've made in the Critical Thinking Chart on the articles you've read. Identify other contrast points. Develop paragraphs discussing those contrasts, and integrate them into your evolving literature review.

14

Differentiating Between Strong and Weak Comparisons and Contrasts

Comparisons and contrasts are most effective when they're strongly related rather than weakly related. That means, rather than try to justify the relationship or closeness of two topics being discussed in your articles, of two outcomes or observations made in your articles, or of two groups involved in the analyses presented in your articles, look for clear associations. Let me give you an example.

Here are seven one-sentence summaries of articles written on globalization.

Article 1: Globalization has resulted in not just factory work being exported, but also in high-tech work being exported.
Article 2: No matter what happens, globalization won't break us because we'll never outsource to other countries our high-level jobs and everyone else can survive on the remaining service jobs.
Article 3: Globalization is changing the nature of fashion within the United States.

Literature Reviews Made Easy, pages 77–81
Copyright © 2010 by Information Age Publishing
All rights of reproduction in any form reserved.

77

Article 4: Globalization has spotlighted a gap between the United States' educational system and those in other countries.

Article 5: In times of crisis, the United States is no longer a nation that could be self-sufficient because many jobs have been exported overseas.

Article 6: As a nation, when we increase our skill levels, globalization will be irrelevant because those who are good at their jobs and hardworking can always find a job in their field of interest.

Article 7: Globalization is causing a loss of good-paying jobs that can be filled by experienced senior citizens strapped financially who lack family able to help them financially.

When looking for comparisons and contrasts, the following articles fit those categories (Table 14.1).

Notice that the two comparison articles state, essentially, that both semiskilled and high technology jobs are being exported, one example of which is the category of jobs normally filled by senior citizens who wish to supplement their incomes. In contrast, the article saying that outsourcing will never occur for pivotal jobs and the article saying that the United States has outsourced too many pivotal jobs disagree with each other. Do you see how the construction of comparisons and contrasts occurs?

TABLE 14.1   Comparison and Contrast Chart

Comparison—drawing similar conclusions	*Contrast*—drawing opposing conclusions
Article 1 and Article 7	Article 2 and Article 5
Globalization has resulted in not just factory work being exported, but also in high-tech work being exported.	No matter what happens globalization won't break us because we'll never outsource to other countries our high-level jobs and everyone else can survive on remaining service jobs.
Globalization is causing a loss of good-paying jobs that can be filled by experienced senior citizens strapped financially who lack family able to help them financially.	In times of crisis, the United States is no longer a nation that could be self-sufficient because many jobs have been exported overseas.

Now, look closely at the list of articles. What other comparisons and contrasts do you see?

If you examine the articles more closely, you can identify how you can build weaker relationships between some of the articles. These relationships are considered weaker because the links between their topics are less direct.

For example, Article 2 and Article 6 both refer to the concept that a number of United States jobs will stay within the country. However, one article refers to high-level jobs and the other article refers to hard workers in jobs at any level.

As a second example, examine Articles 5 and 6, which could loosely be considered as contrasting each other. One suggests that globalization will cripple the country because of the loss of jobs, while the other suggests that regardless of the number of jobs lost the United States will be fine when its citizens are more highly educated.

In both of these cases, the comparison and contrast relationships are weaker because you have to infer a partial connection between these articles to compensate for the absence of exactly matching topics. Those partial connections make the comparisons and contrasts less valuable, since circumstances may not always be right for these relationships to be accurate. In addition, those potential relationship-negating factors must be clearly stated any time the relationships are being discussed. Perhaps most important is the fact that by making the inference required to validate the relationship—comparison or contrast—you as the researcher may be misrepresenting the authors' data, analysis, or conclusions.

TABLE 14.2 Faulty Comparisons

Faulty Comparisons Because Require Inference	Faulty Contrasts Because Require Inference
No matter what happens, globalization won't break us because we'll never outsource to other countries our high-level jobs and everyone else can survive on remaining service jobs.	In times of crisis, the United States is no longer a nation that could be self-sufficient because many jobs have been exported overseas.
As a nation, when we increase our skill levels, globalization will be irrelevant because those who are good at their jobs and hardworking can always find a job in their field of interest.	As a nation, when we increase our skill levels, globalization will be irrelevant because those who are good at their jobs and hardworking can always find a job in their field of interest.

TABLE 14.3   Comparison and Synthesis

Article 4:	Article 6:
Globalization has spotlighted a gap between the United States' educational system and those in other countries.	As a nation, when we increase our skill levels, globalization will be irrelevant because those who are good at their jobs and hardworking can always find a job in their field of interest.

Interestingly, Articles 4 and 6, when linked (Table 14.3), help synthesize a partial picture of American's current economic system.

However, this discussion doesn't cover synthesis. So, the globalization topic will be revisited when synthesis is the focus.

In summary, as you consider the strength of the comparisons and contrasts you create, examine the following:

1. Just how similar are the circumstances you're comparing?
   a. Are the programs, events, or occurrences mirror images of each other?
   b. Are there differences in the environment and, if so, how major are they?
   c. Are there differences in procedures and, if so, how major are they?
   d. Are there differences in the characteristics of participants—staff, observers, participants, evaluators?
   e. Are there differences in the evaluation method and, if so, how major are they?
   f. Are there any other differences that can be identified between the two topics, occurrences, or events that have not been identified here and, if so, how major are they?
2. Just how relevant to each other are these programs, events, circumstances, or occurrences?
   a. Do these programs, events, circumstances, or occurrences each have a perceived purpose?
      i. Who perceives them having a purpose?
      ii. Are the people perceiving them having a purpose the same or different?
   b. How similar or different are their purposes based on people's perceptions or on the nature of the event, circumstance, or occurrence?
   c. How is their purpose perceived by the participants?
3. Are their goals different as a result?

4. Is the mindset within the members of the organization, program, event, circumstance, or occurrence uniformly perceived, or is there variation?
5. Are there differences in time frames for occurrences—phases, patterns, or randomness—that can impact the comparison?
6. Are there any other differences you can identify that would affect how similar the two occurrences, programs, events, or circumstances might be?

When you have completed your consideration of these questions, consider how many of your answers indicate the programs are different from each other. Remember, it's important to understand the nature of similarities between articles first because the more differences you find, the weaker your comparison is. Although for a contrast you want to find differences, if there are too many differences your comparison (similarity) is too weak to express with any certainty.

Why? There may be other factors (variables) impacting your topic about which you know nothing and there may also be relationships with those factors that you are not aware of. In addition, the factors (variables) about which you do know are so large that assigning relative importance to any of them in your examination of your topic is impossible. In other words, your goal is to be able to, like a person preparing yarn to needlepoint, tease out a narrow strand of difference to use in considering the application of the information acquired to your own topic.

So, the concept of narrowing your focus also applies to your comparisons and contrasts. If you have a narrow number of differences to consider, then you can more effectively consider the importance of each.

Practice

Examine all of the comparisons and contrasts you have identified. Consider which are direct and strong and which are loosely related and weak. Eliminate those that are weaker, and develop those that are strong.

Discussion or Writing Assignment

Given the information you've just acquired, examine the comparisons and contrasts you've written and included in the Critical Thinking Chart. After you identify which are strong and weak, either remove weak paragraphs from your literature review or include a description of their strength or weakness in your review.

15

Evaluation of Importance of the Literature to a Topic of Interest

Much of the literature you read will be about your topic but not necessarily directly related. You must, therefore, evaluate that material for relevance and importance to your specific topic and then write an evaluation of that part of the literature that shows how this subtopic is relevant to your main focus and the implications for your topic. If, for example, you're examining tutor-based educational supplement programs for middle school students, you might examine tutor programs for students at different grade levels, parent assistance to students, Sylvan and other specialized programs, or other formal or informal programs. An examination of such programs should include a consideration of how they relate to and explain possible characteristics of your topic—in this case, of tutor-based educational supplement programs for middle school students. By conducting such an evaluation, you gain additional insight into the culture in which your topic functions (such factors as cultural and behavioral expectations, resources available, related programs' designs and dimensions, and other considerations important to your literature review). In other words, evaluations help

Literature Reviews Made Easy, pages 83–86
Copyright © 2010 by Information Age Publishing
All rights of reproduction in any form reserved.
83

you more clearly understand the environment, relevance, and context of your topic.

This ability to evaluate your topic against factors and details found in research-based articles is important for several reasons. First, it gives you a way to compare the value of the information found in your articles, if they are theoretical or represent constructed studies, against your real-life example.

Second, it allows you to evaluate the generalizability of the information you've gathered in your literature search to other situations or circumstances. In the case of an academic literature review, it allows you to evaluate the circumstances you're going to research as part of your dissertation against the general research you're acquiring about the topic. In the case of a simple or applied literature review, it gives you a chance to draw conclusions about your proposed plan or conclusion based on already-experienced and already-analyzed results.

How many evaluations will you have in your literature review? You can have evaluations for each different factor, perspective, or point you're examining about your topic. This can even result in small evaluations of each piece of literature or each grouping of similar articles, if they provide you with valuable insights into your specific situation, event, or program.

For an academic review, the evaluation criteria will be your specific situation, event, or program, as well as your researching environment. With other literature reviews, you may have several evaluation subdivisions or other smaller subgroups to which you apply information in your effort to get a clear picture of the importance of information you've gathered. In such cases, it becomes important to keep the nature of those subgroups in mind sa you both conduct your evaluation and develop your frameworks.

Suppose you're researching the following question: What impact, if any, would a Fortune 500 management training program have on teachers' management effectiveness within their classrooms? There are a number of subquestions to consider when determining the answer. They include:

1. What is known about the role of teachers as managers?
2. What similarities and differences exist between teachers as managers and Fortune 500 business mid-level managers?
3. What training occurs currently for teachers as classroom managers?
4. How effective is the training currently occurring for teachers as classroom managers?
5. What similarities and differences exist between teacher training programs and Fortune 500 business mid-level manager training programs?

Suppose, as another example, you're considering the following question:

> There are a number of useful directions in which to go when creating an evaluation. The choice or choices made will be determined based on ultimate research interests. Here are some possibilities.

1. Compare teaching management to Wal-Mart management methods and needs. (Compare teacher management to management within specific organizations.)
2. Compare Fortune 500 management training programs to management training programs provided by S.C.O.R.E. (Compare Fortune 500 management training to other training programs.)
3. Compare the S.T.E.P. parenting program to teaching management skill requirements.
4. Compare parenting skills to management skills. (Are parenting and management skills different enough to create a need for one over the other?)
5. Compare elementary classroom management training programs with college classroom management training. (Compare classroom needs to different grades.)

By examining this list, you'll see that often evaluation is examining a specific subset related to your larger topic. For an academic literature review, the evaluation would be developed based on the subset or subgroup to which it applied. In other words:

1. What program differences or differences in characteristics can be compared?
2. How are they similar or different? Is there an existing program or occurrence that has the potential to change the characters involved in your topic?
3. Is there a variable involved in one circumstance or occurrence that is not involved in the other that creates the potential for change?
4. If that variable or occurrence can be impacted by human performance of a task, have you factored that potential difference into your evaluation?
5. What characteristics from the external circumstance, program, or event, then, appear to have the ability to positively or negatively impact the specific circumstance you're evaluating?
6. What characteristics from the external circumstance, program, or event remain wild cards?

However, ultimately your smaller evaluations need to be woven together to create a larger framework explaining the larger topic being researched in the study. Put another way, you would narrow your topic to help you identify how the information gathered by others applies to your area of research or program development interest.

Practice

Considering your topic, what areas of interest could you use as evaluation points? Consider the ultimate purpose of your literature review. What evaluation point or points should you use?

Discussion or Writing Activity

1. Examine several of the articles you plan to use. Consider the important information to note about them as you evaluate them against your specific topic (what information is important to better understanding the environment or context of your topic), and include that information on a Critical Thinking Chart like the one in the Appendix. Then draft the evaluation paragraphs for the topics you identified. Integrate those evaluation paragraphs into your evolving literature review.

2. Review the notes you've made in the Critical Thinking Chart on the articles you've read. Identify how other articles relate to your evaluation topic. Develop paragraphs discussing those evaluations, and integrate them into your evolving literature review.

16

Maximizing Your Evaluation

To maximize an evaluation, you need to do two things—consider the content of your evaluation and the placement of your evaluation. These two considerations will be discussed separately here.

Content

First, consider content. Remember, an evaluation is an assessment of what you've learned from the literature in relation to a specific outside topic, circumstance, occurrence, event or phenomenon that you're researching for a particular reason. A careful consideration of the following factors can help you maintain your objectivity and help you link your evaluation solidly to the literature you're reviewing.

As you review these factors, consider your own literature review. Consider how you've used evaluations to relate your research to the specific environment you're examining. Consider whether your logic is presented soundly, and consider whether your logic effectively links your evaluation points to your research topic.

Literature Reviews Made Easy, pages 87–91
Copyright © 2010 by Information Age Publishing
All rights of reproduction in any form reserved.

Using examples to understand these considerations, examine the following. The examples are designed to give you practice in identifying valuable evaluation points.

1. How well linked is your evaluation point?

   This link should be close, not distant. Remember, you want the topics of the research you're evaluating to be closely linked to the topic of your research—the organization, situation, or event. Given that, which of the following topics would be most useful when examining home health care management?

   a. The Home Hospice Program
   b. Physician Office Management
   c. Physician Home Visit Program
   d. Humana Hospital
   e. All Care Hospital Supply

   As you might guess, topics useful for developing evaluation points could be the Home Hospice Program and the Physician Home Visit Program. The office management program, hospital, and hospital supply businesses would be unrelated and would tell you nothing about what your literature really means.

2. How much can the topic of the literature help you evaluate your topic, situation, or event?

   Let's say that you're examining the topic of providing emotional support to clients in home health care programs. Two programs potentially valuable for evaluating your topic in relation to your situation would be the Home Hospice Program and the Physician Home Visit Program. How do you determine which of these is most useful for your evaluation if you're not going to examine either of these topics as a subquestion in your literature review research? You determine which research article (research topic) will give you the best chance to understand the literature in relation to your specific topic. You identify which articles are going to give you different perspectives or insights that help you compare and contrast programs or factors about your topic. In other words, you ask yourself whether some characteristic of the project, situation, or event described in the article is similar to the topic, situation, or event you're researching. Look at each program more closely:

   Home Hospice Program—local independent program, no special management training, no psychologists on staff or as providers, nurses providing service visits in home

Physician Home Visit Program—local independent program, physician oversight for management, psychologists on staff as consultants but not as providers, nurses providing service visits in home, paraprofessionals and medical equipment technicians also providing service

As you can see, there are different facets of each program that may be potentially helpful. The Home Hospice Program has faculty with no special psychology training, so it might be useful as a counter perspective article that illustrates what can happen when no individuals trained in providing emotional support are involved in providing health services. However, the value of the article will probably be limited, since the patients' emotional needs may not be the focus of the article and little may be said about emotional needs.

It is much more likely that you will get some input from the Physician Home Visit Program because it has psychologists for consultation with the staff. Since the interest is emotional support provided by home health care providers, the maximal opportunity to consider variables would appear to be the Physician Home Visit Program.

However, the final decision will be based on exactly what is available in the literature. If the literature doesn't discuss medical technicians in any detail, it might prove less beneficial to choose the Physician Home Visit Program because no beneficial information would be available on what they could mean to patients needing emotional support. On the other hand, if clients' emotional needs are discussed in the Home Hospice Program, then it may prove to be the more useful article.

Having chosen the evaluation point you're going to search for comparison in the literature you're reading, the next step is to compare the dynamics in the literature to see how similar or different they are from the situation or event you're specifically trying to understand. That similarity or difference would include:

1. whether there's information on the characteristics quality providers should have
2. whether there's information on medical technicians' roles in patient interactions, on physicians' home visit roles in patient interactions, and on nurses' roles in patient interactions
3. whether there's information on the emotional support provided by home health care providers that impacts your choice of program to explore

In other words, is there any information, either because a provided program or training proved helpful, or none was provided and there was some observation that additional emotional support would prove helpful to clients? If there is such information, then the article can help you assess the need for emotional support and what's required to provide it. If not, then the value of the article to your evaluation is limited.

So, having analyzed an article or group of articles and conducted a comparison and contrast of them, you would use that comparison and contrast to better understand the relationship of the information to your topic and your specific situation or event. In this case, that information would include the characteristics of home health care providers' emotional support of home-bound patients in relation to the special needs of your selected program.

Placement

Second, consider placement of your evaluation. For each major (and many minor) point you consider in your literature review, you'll want to include an evaluation of it in relation to your topic. Placement of that information can be important to your readers' understanding of your topic and the points you make.

Although your evaluations could be placed in a number of places, two might be considered most obvious. The first would be at the end of all comparisons and contrasts as part of the synthesis and integration. The second would be at the end of your discussion of each major comparison and contrast point. However, in a well-developed literature review, the evaluation will often exist in both.

As a continuation of your logical presentation of research and conclusions drawn about that research, presenting evaluations at the end of your consideration of each major point allows the importance and strength of your conclusions to be evident to readers. Repeated briefly as part of the creation of your synthesis and integration, evaluations create logic bridges from your initial consideration of each point to your conclusions about the importance of those points to your topic and your "next step." Their repetition also allows the reader to understand why you draw the conclusions that dictate the characteristics of your synthesis and integration.

Practice

Re-examine your list of evaluation points. Evaluate which provide the most direct opportunities for you to provide comparisons and contrasts based on your question and topic.

Discussion or Writing Assignment

Given the information you've just acquired, examine the evaluations you've written and included in the Critical Thinking Chart. After you identify which are direct or weaker, either remove weaker paragraphs from your literature review or include a description of their strengths or weaknesses in your literature review.

17

How Does Synthesizing Ideas Create a Framework?

For a moment, picture synthesizing ideas as similar to creating a spider web that explains information and insights on a specific topic. Synthesis is just such a spider web. Its action is like weaving together the agreeing, complementary ideas of different researchers to create a whole picture of how different pieces of research support each other.

Here's an example. You have 12 articles whose one-sentence to two-sentence summaries follow:

Article 1: A randomly selected group of teenagers in an urban school district have no interest in higher education because they believe they will not live to see their 20th birthday.

Article 2: Randomly selected middle school students in three urban school districts are concerned about their futures and interested in becoming involved in training programs and college after graduating.

Literature Reviews Made Easy, pages 93–98
Copyright © 2010 by Information Age Publishing
All rights of reproduction in any form reserved.

Article 3: An ethnographic examination in three rural school districts demonstrates that rural teenagers tend to leave their communities to go to college.

Article 4: Randomly selected rural high school students in one state indicated they find college a good way to escape what they feel to be the negative aspects of their rural environment.

Article 5: Randomly selected low income urban high school students indicated they believed college was their chance to escape the poverty in which they were living.

Article 6: High school students' high stakes testing in one state indicate that 65% of the students' scores were not high enough to graduate from high school, or indicate they might be accepted in a 4-year college.

Article 7: Approximately 85% of urban high school students' high stakes testing scores in three urban districts were high enough for students to pass, and those scores indicate they should be accepted to a 4-year college.

Article 8: Randomly selected rural high school students in three districts indicated they find their environment boring and that college is one way to escape their environment.

Article 9: Randomly selected urban high school students in three schools indicate they find their environment limiting and want to find a new challenge. They indicated college offered them one opportunity to pursue other interests.

Article 10: Approximately 50% of randomly selected urban high school students believed they would never succeed in high school, so they shouldn't try.

Article 11: Approximately 35% of randomly selected middle school students in three districts believed high school would be difficult emotionally and cognitively, but they felt ready for the challenge.

Article 12: Approximately 70% of randomly selected high school high income district students indicated their parents would be disappointed with them if they didn't go to college, so no other post-secondary school options appeared worth considering.

To synthesize these ideas, examine each to see which don't contradict each other. You could sort them this way:

Wish to go to college:

Article 2, 11 middle school students
Article 3, 4, 8 rural high school students

Article 5 urban low income high school students
Article 9 urban high school students
Article 12 high income high school students
Article 1 teenagers

All of these articles report findings about whether or why students want to go to college. How then do you synthesize them? You look at the piece of the picture that each individual article can add to an overall view of why students want to go to college. Remember, you always start with an overview or introduction of your topic. So, your synthesis of ideas might look like this:

> When considering motivations and impediments to middle and high school students attending college, a number of studies provide insight. Smith (2004), using a random survey of a large middle school sample, determined students in the sample believed they could accomplish whatever they set out to do, although completing college might prove cognitively and emotionally challenging. Alexander (2008) further found, when conducting a case study on middle school motivations for attending college, that a number of such participants believed attending college would be a logical part of their process for accomplishing their goals since it would allow them to develop the background required. Jones (2003), also, found when conducting a phenomenological study of the planning process rural high school students used to determine post-high school activities, found one reason such students decided to attend college was because they found life in their rural communities boring. Both Jeffries (2001) and Davis (2004), conducting similar case studies of rural high school students in two different locations, also determined such students liked to attend college, although their participants indicated key to their decision making was, respectively, a belief their rural environments had negative aspects and a belief college held challenges they welcomed. Similar to Jones (2003), Germaine (2005), found in a randomized survey of high school students in three major urban areas that urban students also indicated they wished to attend college because they were bored. In addition, Kauffman (2006) found results similar to Alexander (2008) when he determined in a phenomenology examining a small urban high school student sample that participants saw it as their chance to achieve their goal of escaping poverty. Finally, high income high school students examined in a multiple case study by Crane (2005) expressed another reason for attending college—the desire to not disappoint their parents. In fact, they believed that there was no other acceptable option.

Do you see how each of these pieces contributes to creating part of a spider web that explains reasons high school students may select college?

Now it's time to revisit the globalization example used earlier in the discussion of comparisons and contrasts.

Here are 7 one-sentence summaries for articles on globalization.

Article 1: Globalization has resulted in not just factory work being exported, but also in high-tech work being exported.

Article 2: No matter what happens, globalization won't break us because we'll never outsource to other countries our high-level jobs and everyone else can survive on remaining service jobs.

Article 3: Globalization is changing the nature of fashion within the United States.

Article 4: Globalization has spotlighted a gap between the United States' educational system and those in other countries.

Article 5: In times of crisis, the United States is no longer a nation that could be self-sufficient because many jobs have been exported overseas.

Article 6: As a nation, when we increase our skill levels, globalization will be irrelevant because those who are good at their jobs and hardworking can always find a job in their field of interest.

Article 7: Globalization is causing a loss of good-paying jobs that can be filled by experienced senior citizens strapped financially who lack family able to help them financially.

When developing syntheses, once again, you review the information you've formulated on comparisons to see how those pieces of information can fit together to explain different dimensions of the same topic (Table 17.1).

Articles 1 and 7 reinforce each other. Combined, they explain that factory and high-tech work is being exported. They also explain that loss of jobs in the U.S. is causing a loss of income to senior citizens who are on their own. Together, this explains the type of work being lost and one reason why that type of work is important.

TABLE 17.1   Comparison and Conclusions

Comparison—*Article 1 and Article 7*

Comparison—drawing similar conclusions

Globalization has resulted in not just factory work being exported, but also in high-tech work being exported.

Globalization is causing a loss of good-paying jobs that can be filled by experienced senior citizens strapped financially who lack family able to help them financially.

TABLE 17.2 Synthesizing Partial Pictures

Article 4:	Article 6:
Globalization has spotlighted a gap between the United States' educational system and those in other countries.	As a nation, when we increase our skill levels, globalization will be irrelevant because those who are good at their jobs and hardworking can always find a job in their field of interest.

Interestingly, articles 4 and 6 help to synthesize a partial picture of American's current economic system (Table 17.2).

What Does This Mean?

Globalization has spotlighted a gap between educational systems in the United States and other countries. Once the skill levels of our citizens have been raised to bridge that gap, no more jobs will be lost to globalization because Americans will have enough skills for the nation to maintain high employment rates.

Can you see how syntheses fit together? The articles contain slightly different information that, when combined by recognizing similarities, creates a more complete picture.

Before moving on, it's important to discuss being careful when creating syntheses. During the process of creating syntheses, researchers are building conclusions based on the linking (or weaving together) of multiple ideas. This is a point where faulty logic, inappropriately understood or applied information, inaccurately understood or applied information, or overgeneralization can cause fatal errors in the development of a sound literature review. Since a literature review is used to develop a theoretical framework for further research or project development, it's essential to be rigorous in examining literature and data during this synthesis process.

Practice

Examine the comparison points you've developed from your literature search. Which have the same or similar topics? Consider how they can be woven together to explain your circumstance or topic.

Discussion or Writing Activity

Examine several of the articles you plan to use. Consider the important information to note about them as you examine your comparisons of them in the Critical Thinking Chart.

Consider how those comparisons fit together to create a larger picture of your topic. Record those relationships in the Critical Thinking Chart.

18

What Does a Synthesis Look Like?

Syntheses look different from the comparisons to which they are closely related. The reason is that comparisons might be made between the characteristics of, or results reported, in one or several articles. Syntheses reach a step farther to look at larger instances of commonality. Here are some examples of what a synthesis might look like.

Example 1—a synthesis presentation dissected. The first example below presented uses the factors or characteristics considered in the previous chapter. This example considered reasons high school students go to college. First, you determine the different factors your examination of research indicated are reasons high school students go to college. Then, you combine them into agreeing and complementary pieces of information that explain your topic and in part your specific situation or event. What would such a synthesis of agreeing and complementary pieces of information look like? Here's one possibility:

> Numerous reasons were identified for high school students electing to attend college. Numbers of both rural and urban high school students indi-

Literature Reviews Made Easy, pages 99–103
Copyright © 2010 by Information Age Publishing
All rights of reproduction in any form reserved.

cated they were bored with their environments and saw college attendance as a chance to experience new challenges (Jeffries, 2001; Davis, 2004; Jermaine, 2005). In addition, urban low income students saw college as an opportunity to escape poverty (Kauffman, 2006). High income high school students indicated a third motivation—the desire to please their parents (Crane, 2005).

Notice that, in this paragraph, the focus is on *how these pieces fit together to create an overall picture* of what is known. From that group of articles, this illustrates how the reasons for high school students' motivation to attend college can be combined. Notice the reasons that students did not go to college are not addressed. The specific groups involved in each of these motivations are identified.

Do rural low income students wish to escape poverty? Perhaps, and that could be discussed in a separate paragraph within your literature review as information that should be considered in future research. However, that information isn't discussed in the literature you've read for your review, so it isn't included in the synthesis.

The literature that's relevant is cited. That's important, since this part of the literature review creates a framework for future research or activities. Why is the framework you develop important? Whether the literature review is simple, applied, or academic, it provides the basis for any conclusions made or future plans created. It is the justification for your *money* if you write a grant proposal, your *proposed action plan* if you conduct a case study, your *research study* if you defend a dissertation proposal, or your *conclusions* if you write a simple literature review. So, although the articles were cited earlier as they were considered and discussed, they should be cited in the synthesis so that readers can continue to understand the line of logic being created by you, the writer. Otherwise, your literature review may end with a whimper rather than a bang.

Notice also that the verbs in this paragraph are in past tense—were, saw, indicated. The standard for writing about most articles used in a literature review is past tense. After all, each of the articles being read has been written in the past. So, each of the research studies done to gather the information shared in those articles was done in the past.

The one exception to this past tense would be sharing something that is meant to be a generalizable, ongoing conclusion. For example: *Piaget (1955) determined that infants experience separation anxiety from about 6 months old to 1 year old.*

This statement does not describe a specific study, its results, or the conclusions drawn from it. Instead, it describes an ongoing conclusion generalizable to a specific group, regardless of the period of time in which it's occurring.

Example 2—the use of syntheses as links and literature review developmental steps. It's also important to understand how syntheses can occur in multiple locations throughout the literature review. By developing syntheses at different points in the review, you allow readers to gain ever increasing understandings of the relationship between different factors involved in your topic and their importance to the complex, complete picture.

Let's look at a couple of other syntheses to illustrate this. Synthesis 1:

> Although students of all ages are affected by the diversification within Utah's evolving cultural environment, adolescence is the period when children are most likely to confront, be able to respond to, and actually incorporate alternative lifestyles, alternative world views, and new friendship choices (Stryker, 1980). Their exposures to those different attitudes and life choices can affect their identity development. The greater their adherence to the behaviors, norms, and values expected by the groups with which they associate, the greater the salience of their role identities (Burke & Reitzes, 1991). The greater their experimentation with the different behavior, norm, and value options they are presented, the less the salience. This experimentation can result in identity confusion and ambiguity. Further, adolescence is the period during which children separate from their families, in part by differentiating their knowledge and what they care about from that which their parents know and care about (Cornwall, 1989; Youniss & Ketterlinus, 1987). (Dawidowicz, 2001, p. 20–21)

This synthesis serves as a part of the conclusions at the end of a section of the literature review. Farther into the dissertation is the following.

> The role of the family is the socialization of each of its members. As individuals within the family interact, each member learns certain behavior patterns that tend to be used or modified in future interactions. To completely recreate these patterns proves difficult at best, so identification of and understanding of both the various circumstances that create patterns and the likely patterns these circumstances can cause become essential (Balcom, Lee, & Tager, 1995; Baumrind, 1991; Ford, 1992; Knudson-Martin, 1994; Meyerstein, 1996; Small & Eastman, 1991). (Dawidowicz, 2001, p. 22)

Notice that there are no citations here. Because this information is woven from data discussed directly before this synthesis, the writer does not cite that information. Instead, the citation is presented in context previously and synthesized here.

Example 3—syntheses in articles you read. This following synthesis is in-cluded to show that syntheses do not always occur during the literature review sections of articles you read. Syntheses will be integral to interpret-ing and analyzing any data, and are something you will see as you read any article. It's good to recognize their use and be a critical reader of them, since faulty logic here can create poorly drawn conclusions. In this case, the synthesis is part of the creation of a research framework at the beginning of an article.

> Although some students entered the school because they preferred its edu-cational schedule, the program used became an important benefit to many students because its democratic teaching techniques could help combat their feelings of inadequacy and unacceptance. Instead, it could contribute to their development of positive self-esteem, positive school experiences, and improved school performance. Some of these techniques included the use of first names, equal treatment, and active listening employing equal teacher and student respect (Bynum & Dunn, 1996; Dawidowicz, 2001; Field, Lang, Yando, & Bendell, 1995; Gay, 1988; Haensley & Parsons, 1993; Ho, Lempers & Clark-Lempers, 1995; Hoge, Smit, & Crist, 1997; Jacobvitz & Bush, 1996; Levendosky, Okun & Parker, 1995; McCabe, 1997; Liu, Kaplan, & Risser, 1992; Rabow, Radcliffe-Vasile, Newcomb, & Hernandez, 1992; Roizblatt et al., 1997; Schechtman, 1993; Sheets et al., 1996; Speicher, 1994; Whitbeck, Hoyt, Miller & Kao, 1992; Wilson & Wilson, 1992).

This portion of a synthesis is presented to explain the initial theoretical framework used to design and conduct a study. It is similar to the synthesis found at the end of a literature review in a dissertation or at the end of the theoretical framework section of an article presenting a study.

Note that all three of these syntheses are summary in nature. Syntheses are summaries because they combine information already discussed earlier in the literature review or drawing together already analyzed information from other literature reviews. Further, in two of the three examples there are citations, and those citations identify the articles used to create a theo-retical framework.

> Again, as you synthesize data or review the syntheses of others, be sure you watch the logic trail being created. Also pay attention to whether you see any misinterpretation or misrepresentation of data. Whether intentional or unintentional, such errors can create fatal flaws in a literature review.

Practice

After having identified the points you will include in your synthesis, consider where you're placing this synthesis in your literature review or article. Do you need citations? How should you develop it? Draft at least one synthesis for your literature review.

Discussion or Writing Activity

Having examined the Critical Thinking Chart and identified the relationships of comparisons that form a larger picture of your topic, draft synthesis paragraphs for the potential places where syntheses are needed. Place those synthesis paragraphs into your evolving literature review.

Reference

Dawidowicz, P. (2001). *"Sometimes you gotta learn the concept, not just the rules": Educational and cultural impacts of Utah's diversification process.* Ann Arbor, MI: UMI Press.

19

Synthesis and Integration: Complementing Ideas

Integration complements synthesis because it's the process of finding a way to make seemingly contradictory ideas form some type of logical complementary picture. What, you say? What does that mean? It means seeing how one circumstance studied differs from another to identify why the results of what on the surface appear to be two identically designed studies or circumstances might yield completely different results. By identifying those differences, it's possible to reconcile varying results and understand how the studies or observations fit together to explain the dynamics of a complex topic.

Let's look at the articles we used in the example of synthesis in the last chapter.

Article 1: A randomly selected group of teenagers in an urban school district have no interest in higher education because they believe they will not live to see their 20th birthday.

Literature Reviews Made Easy, pages 105–109
Copyright © 2010 by Information Age Publishing
All rights of reproduction in any form reserved. **105**

Article 2: Randomly selected middle school students in three urban school districts are concerned about their futures and interested in becoming involved in training programs and college after graduating.

Article 3: An ethnographic examination of literature in three rural school districts demonstrates that rural teenagers tend to leave their communities to go to college.

Article 4: Randomly selected rural high school students in one state indicated they find college a good way to escape what they feel to be the negative aspects of their rural environment.

Article 5: Randomly selected low income urban high school students indicated they believed college was their chance to escape the poverty in which they were living.

Article 6: High school students' high stakes testing in one state indicate that 65% of the students' scores were not high enough to graduate from high school or be accepted in a 4-year college.

Article 7: Approximately 85% of urban high school students' high stakes testing scores in three urban districts were high enough for students to pass, and those scores indicate they should be accepted to a 4-year college.

Article 8: Randomly selected rural high school students in three districts indicated they find their environment boring and that college is one way to escape their environment.

Article 9: Randomly selected urban high school students in three schools indicate they find their environment limiting and want to find a new challenge. They indicated college offered them one opportunity to pursue other interests.

Article 10: Approximately 50% of randomly selected urban high school students believed they would never succeed in high school, so they shouldn't try.

Article 11: Approximately 35% of randomly selected middle school students in three districts believed high school would be difficult emotionally and cognitively, but they felt ready for the challenge.

Article 12: Approximately 70% of randomly selected high school high income district students indicated their parents would be disappointed with them if they didn't go to college, so no other postsecondary school options appeared worth considering.

As you can see from the difference in font, contradictory articles appear to be:

Article 1: majority of urban teenagers in one district did not want college, did not believe they would live to their 20th birthdays

Article 6: 65% students' scores not high enough to get accepted to college

Article 10: 50% of randomly selected urban high school students felt would never succeed in high school, so why try

Let's look back at the synthesis to see how the contradictory articles can fit into the total picture. Based on the fictitious articles, here's the previous synthesis:

> Numerous reasons were identified for high school students electing to attend college. Both numbers of rural and urban high school students indicated they were bored with their environments and saw college attendance as a chance to experience new challenges (Jeffries, 2001; Davis, 2004; Jermaine, 2005). In addition, urban low income students saw college as an opportunity to escape poverty (Kauffman, 2006). High income high school students indicated a third motivation—the desire to please their parents (Crane, 2005).

Now to add the integration:

> However, in some urban locations, it appears the majority of teenagers indicated they did not believe they would live until they were 20 years old. As a result, they felt college was not worth pursuing (Anwat, 2001). Perhaps for students in particularly violent urban locations, a sense of overwhelming danger discourages planning for the future. At the same time, students who did not receive high enough test scores and high school grades to get accepted into college might also become discouraged and choose not to pursue college, even if they can access alternative higher education entrance methods (Verdun, 2003). This is perhaps borne out by a study indicating 50% of urban high school students felt they would never succeed in high school (Blaine, 2005).

As a second example, here are 7 one-sentence summaries for articles on globalization.

Article 1: Globalization has resulted in not just factory work being exported, but also in high-tech work being exported.

Article 2: No matter what happens, globalization won't break us because we'll never outsource to other countries our high-level jobs and everyone else can survive on remaining service jobs.

Article 3: Globalization is changing the nature of fashion within the
United States.

Article 4: Globalization has spotlighted a gap between the United
States' educational system and those in other countries.

Article 5: In times of crisis, the United States is no longer a nation that
could be self-sufficient because many jobs have been exported
overseas.

Article 6: As a nation, when we increase our skill levels, globalization
will be irrelevant because those who are good at their jobs and
hardworking can always find a job in their field of interest.

Article 7: Globalization is causing a loss of good-paying jobs that can be
filled by experienced senior citizens strapped financially who lack
family able to help them financially.

When looking for comparisons and contrasts, the articles in Table 19.1
fit those categories.

Article 6 could also loosely be considered as contrasting these two articles. One suggests that globalization will cripple the country because of the
loss of jobs, while the other suggests that regardless of the number of jobs
lost, the United States be fine when its citizens are more highly educated.

The integration could be explained like this:

Although the country is no longer self-sufficient because of the loss of jobs,
globalization will never break the country because the United States will
never outsource high-level jobs to other countries. As long as high-level jobs
are maintained, everyone not in a high level job can survive on the remaining service level jobs, regardless of which jobs have been lost overseas. Finally, although a number of jobs have gone overseas, more jobs will become
available as individuals' skill levels increase and jobs are returned to the
country as a result.

TABLE 19.1 Contrasting Chart

Contrast—Article 2 and Article 5

Contrast: drawing opposing conclusions

No matter what happens, globalization won't break us because we'll never
outsource to other countries our high-level jobs and everyone else can survive
on remaining service jobs.

In times of crisis, the United States is no longer a nation that could be self-
sufficient because many jobs have been exported overseas.

Notice how these different, almost contradictory ideas can be combined to create a whole that explains how these different articles fit together rather than contradict each other.

Remember, as you develop your integrations, that citing your sources is important. Just as with your development of syntheses, you need to support your sources effectively here to guarantee your integrations carry the weight they deserve.

Before moving on, it's important to discuss being careful when creating integrations. During the process of creating integrations, researchers are building conclusions based on the linking (or weaving together) of multiple ideas. This is a point where faulty logic, inaccurately understood or applied information, or overgeneralization can cause fatal errors in the development of a sound literature review. Since a literature review is used to develop a theoretical framework for further research or project development, it's essential to be rigorous in examining literature and data during this integration process.

Practice

Examine the contrasts you identified in previous work on your topic. How can these contrasts be combined to explain and complement each other even though they appear to be contradictions of each other?

Discussion or Writing Activity

Examine several of the articles you plan to use. Consider the important information to note about them as you examine your contrasts of them in the Critical Thinking Chart. Consider how those contrasts fit together to create a larger picture of your topic. Record those relationships in the Critical Thinking Chart.

Having examined the Critical Thinking Chart and identified the relationships of contrasts that form a larger picture of your topic, draft paragraphs for the integrations you've identified. Place those integration paragraphs into your evolving literature review.

20

Analysis, Comparison, Contrast, Evaluation, Synthesis, and Integration

Does it feel like you just keep examining the data over and over again? Where does synthesis fit in relation to analysis, comparison, contrast, and evaluation? Let's look at the relationship and make the process feel a little less repetitive.

The process of examination of data using higher order thinking skills is actually in itself composed of an interconnecting set of activities. Analysis of each article takes place. Based on that analysis, a determination is made about the value of each article to the literature review.

Articles selected as valuable are used to form comparisons and contrasts. Those article analyses and comparisons and contrasts are used to create both the syntheses and integrations of information to create frameworks. Finally, evaluation of articles individually, of comparisons and contrasts, and of syntheses and integrations are all used as part of the process of evaluating your literature against the specific situation or event you are ultimately examining. This applies to all literature reviews, whether they're

Literature Reviews Made Easy, pages 111–113
Copyright © 2010 by Information Age Publishing
All rights of reproduction in any form reserved.

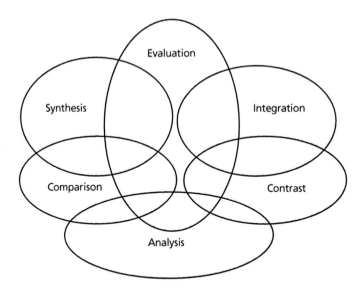

Figure 20.1 The parts of a literature review.

developed to design an action plan of some type or to develop a research study design. More will be said about this shortly.

A pictorial diagram of the relationships between different parts of a literature review is displayed in Figure 20.1.

As this figure indicates, synthesis and integration act as a culmination of the assessment done throughout a literature review. While developing them, researchers who have examined literature from multiple perspectives create an overall picture of a generic environment similar to the environment in which their topic's situation or event occurs. This allows researchers to create the theoretical framework that helps them determine where to start when planning for a program or study of their specific situations.

At the same time, synthesis and integration allow researchers like you to evaluate what is known about their topic in relation to their specific situation or event. By evaluating everything they read for its applicability to their specific situation, they optimize their opportunity to either develop a proposal for action (simple or applied literature review) or develop a strong justification for the study they will conduct (academic literature review).

What is the point? None of the critical thinking skills or processes can stand alone. You must apply them all effectively and realistically to the information you acquire to create a sound literature review.

So, although your literature review can feel like numerous repetitions of examination of the same material, each of these steps looks at the information in a slightly different framework. This use of different lenses to consider the same information helps build the objectivity of your literature review. It also helps you build your information logically to develop an ever larger picture of the information you're gathering.

Practice

Re-examine your comparisons, contrasts, and evaluations. Have you missed any synthesis or integration points you might otherwise have included in your literature review? If you have, develop them now.

Discussion or Writing Activity

Read your literature review as it stands now. Recognizing that it's probably still a work in progress, consider how it reads at this point. Identify whether any of your analyses, comparisons, contrasts, evaluations, syntheses, and integrations contradict other materials. If so, consider how to reconcile these materials. Alter your Critical Thinking Chart and literature review draft appropriately.

21

Organizing Your Assessment of the Literature

It may seem strange to be considering this when you have already written your outline much earlier in this process. However, that outline should be a living organism that can change as a result of your research. Although you had some basic ideas about what you wanted to cover and in what order, often the available information is different and calls for changes in your outline. In addition, as you identify the syntheses and integrations that create your framework, you may identify a different method of organizing your review that will make it clearer and more effective. So, reviewing and organizing your literature review at this point is desirable because you can evaluate the relative usefulness of different organizational methods based on the information you have to share.

Some people believe that, when writing literature reviews, writers should examine each article in order. Using this theory, examination and analysis of all of the articles should be presented in the first section. Following that, all of the comparisons and contrasts should be presented. Synthe-

Literature Reviews Made Easy, pages 115–119
Copyright © 2010 by Information Age Publishing
All rights of reproduction in any form reserved.
115

TABLE 21.1 Organizational Plans for Literature Reviews

Table of Contents 1:	Table of Contents 2:	Table of Contents 3:
Introduction	Introduction	Introduction
Analysis of Literature	Ages 1–5	Parents' Roles (This represents examination point 1.)
Comparison and Contrast	Ages 6–10	Teachers' Roles (This represents examination point 2.)
Evaluation Against My Special Topic	Ages 11–14	Community's Roles (This represents examination point 3.)
Synthesis and Integration of Literature	Ages 15–20	Students' Roles (This represents examination point 4.)
Conclusions	Adulthood	Synthesis and Integration
	Synthesis and Integration	Conclusions
	Conclusions	

ses and integrations should come next, and should be followed, finally, by evaluations and conclusions.

That type of paper presentation can be used, but it can limit your ability to present arguments effectively. To consider how your thinking can be presented, let's look at several different layouts for tables of contents (Table 21.1).

As you can see, you can organize your essay to make your research most understandable by your readers. You can organize simply by type of work you will be doing (column 2) or become more sophisticated to present timeframes thought to impact your focus as in column 2 (good for some examinations of human development) or by significant factors (good for any number of topics or questions).

Let's look at each in a little more detail here.

Table of Contents 1 presents an example of separating different higher order thinking skills so that readers can follow the information logically and easily. It is a good basic structure. Each piece of information can be easily identified and presented so that you, the writer, can make sure you've made all of your points. This version of a table of contents is always acceptable, but there are times when it can actually be a drawback. Let's look at Table of Contents 2 to understand some of those drawbacks.

Table of Contents 2 separates information being examined by periods based on time. This is good when handling information that applies to different physical or geographic ages or different periods in history. This type of organization let's you, the writer, separate information dealing with a specific period from information about another specific period. What does that mean? When you provide information that cuts across ages or time periods and that information is organized thinking skill type (column 1), it's easy to get confused about what's supposed to happen in what stage or time period. In such cases where timelines are important, it can be easier for readers and, as a result, for you when the information provided is dealt with by time frame. At the end, conclusions based on synthesis and integration of information can be presented either by specific period or with all ages or time periods included.

Table of Contents 3 separates information in the literature review by the groups of individuals being discussed. The benefit to this type of design is that it's easier for both you and readers to identify the relative roles and variations in character and the impact of the different groups being considered. Again, if the information were presented using the design used in Table of Contents 1, readers would have to shift their attention between the different groups. That shifting between groups for first analysis, then comparison and contrast, and so on, can make it harder to follow the logic used when considering each individual group. In other words, sorting information by group lets the reader understand all of the characteristics of each group before moving on to the next group.

There are several other methods of organization possible. They are considered here.

- A first is organizing your literature review based on *trends*. Organization by trend involves organizing articles, comparisons, and contrasts to consider trends that are identified as evolving in the literature. This could include management trends, trends in behaviors, trends in responses to stimuli, or analysis trends.
- A second is organizing your literature review based on the *themes* you identify in your literature. Using this method, you would sort your information based on topics. Topics could be groups, as described above (i.e., family, community, school, or gang) or organizational structure (i.e., system, individual, neighborhood, community, or state). It could include diseases, treatments, and cures.

Your selection of this organizational method depends in large part upon the question with which you began. In other words, if you identify themes based on the size of a group being examined but also identify that size has little to do with differentiating results or sharing important information, you shouldn't use it as an organizational theme. You thus change your themes as you do your review.

▪ A third organizational method would be sorting information by research methods used. Those methods might become important if you feel the methods made a difference in results. In most examinations not directly related to methodology, this would be an organizational method subsumed in a larger organizational structure. In other words, your organization is by group.

Your groups might be:

1. parents
2. teenagers
3. children
4. grandparents

You might find that results are different based on the research method used:

1. statistical analyses
2. interviews, questionnaires, and observations
3. quasi-experimental and experimental studies

Your organization might look like this:

1. Parents
   a. Statistical analysis
   b. Interviews, questionnaires, and observations
   c. Quasi-experimental and experimental studies
2. Teenagers
   a. Statistical analysis
   b. Interviews, questionnaires, and observations
   c. Quasi-experimental and experimental studies
3. Children
   a. Statistical analysis
   b. Interviews, questionnaires, and observations
   c. Quasi-experimental and experimental studies

4. Grandparents
   a. Statistical analysis
   b. Interviews, questionnaires, and observations
   c. Quasi-experimental and experimental studies

Which organizational model is the correct model for your literature review? It depends on what you're examining and how you can most clearly present your information. Does your material lend itself to a discussion of trends, of time periods or themes, of authors' or theorists' perspectives, or of research methodused? Remember, Table of Contents 1 will never be wrong. However, it will often not be the easiest model for both you and your readers to understand.

Practice

Using the information you will present in your literature review, re-examine your initial literature review outline. Consider the assessment results you've identified. Restructure your outline to reflect the table of contents model that will present your information most effectively.

Discussion or Writing Activity

Reorganize your material using the organizational method you've selected. In addition, consider your headers and the transitions you need to develop to make the literature review most effective.

22

Separating Your Ideas from Authors' Ideas

The authors you read will make observations, comparisons and contrasts, syntheses and integrations, and evaluations, just as you will. Some of them will be important to share in your literature review. If you share that information correctly, your literature review will be stronger. If you share that information incorrectly, your literature review will be confusing, because the reader will be unable to differentiate between your ideas and those of the author whose thoughts you're paraphrasing.

Sharing your thoughts incorrectly in your literature review can even cause others to question your integrity if they believe you're attributing your thoughts to the author whose work you're paraphrasing. If that's the case, your readers can believe you're attempting to bias or falsely represent the information you've read to support your own agenda.

So, how do you keep your ideas and your authors' ideas separate without using first person to make comments like, "I conclude, I believe, or I notice" or awkward comments like, "the author concludes, believes, or

Literature Reviews Made Easy, pages 121–124
Copyright © 2010 by Information Age Publishing
All rights of reproduction in any form reserved.

notices?" There are several ways you can accomplish it. Examples follow for your review and evaluation.

Example 1:

> Smith (2004) says brownies are the most addictive substance in the world. Based on the Standards for Avoiding Addiction, this study indicates brownies should be avoided. There are inconsistencies in the analysis, though.

Note that in this example, there is no separation of the article's substance and the writer's ideas. Was the comment on the Standards for Avoiding Addiction part of Smith's study, or was it the writer's idea? Was everything shared by Smith cited, or could some of Smith's ideas been credited instead to the writer?

Example 2:

> Brownies have been found to be the most addictive substances in the world. In fact, using the Standards for Avoiding Addiction, people should avoid eating brownies (Smith, 2004, p. 23). However, there appear to be inconsistencies in the data analysis of the study drawing those conclusions.

Note that this version is acceptable. By placing the Smith citation between the article's information and the writer's observations, the two pieces of information are easily identified as separate and by author. Note, though, that there could be confusion about the placement of the page number in the citation. Because it cites the source of all information presented before it, the page number should only be presented in that manner when all information shared appears on page 29 in the original text.

Example 3:

> Smith (2004) stated that brownies are the most addictive substance in the world. Based on this information, Smith determined that the Standards for Avoiding Addiction dictates people should avoid eating brownies (p. 23). However, inconsistencies in the analysis of brownies' addictiveness raise questions about Smith's conclusions.

Note that this version is acceptable. First, it identifies that the initial information provided comes from an article written by Smith in 2004. Second, it provides the page number from which the information provided was drawn. That page number also separates Smith's ideas from the writer's. Finally, it cites Smith as separate from the observation being made.

Let's examine one more set of examples. Watch for the pattern.

Example 1:

> Once every 15 years, locusts come out and ravage the population. They can devastate the land. It appears they can do more damage than Agent Orange. These locusts can eat 17 times their body weight (Smith, 2004).

Note that in this case both facts provided by the Smith (2004) and the author's thoughts on those facts are intermingled in this paragraph. Unlike the first set of examples where the author being discussed was cited first, here the author is cited last. However, the lack of separation between the cited author's and researcher's comments makes this paragraph ineffective.

Example 2:

> Based on current research on locusts, it appears they may be more damaging than Agent Orange. According to this research, once every 15 years locusts hatch that eat 17 times their body weight daily before dying at the end of their life cycles, some 30 days later (Smith, 2004, ¶ 23).

Note that this example is technically acceptable because it identifies the point where research paraphrasing begins—where the phrase *according to this research* is used. However, it can still be confusing. Did Smith develop the comparison between locusts and Agent Orange?

Example 3:

> "Once every 15 years, locusts hatch that eat 17 times their body weight daily before dying themselves 30 days later" (Smith, 2004, ¶ 23). Based on this information, it would appear locusts could be more damaging to local foliage than the application of Agent Orange.

Note that this is the best separation of the authors' and researchers' ideas. It presents the information, just as in the other examples, at the beginning of the paragraph. It places the citation between paraphrased information and the writer's ideas. It uses appropriate words like *seems, appears,* and *is possible* to differentiate between information presented by the cited author and the conjectures, illustrations, and observations made by the writer.

Practice

Review the draft of your literature review. Identify any areas where readers might not be clear about your comments and the comments of the authors you have read. For those areas, rewrite those materials.

Discussion or Writing Activity

Consider any new applications you can identify using your comparison, contrast, evaluation, synthesis, and integration skills. Expand your work to include those new points.

23

Peer Critiquing

If you're creating a literature review for a dissertation, you have a committee that can act as peer critiquers to help you improve your work. In other situations, you might be able to find someone who can give you feedback. If that's the case, often that person will also be the one who defines how the review is conducted and what information the feedback supplied provides.

If you have the chance to encourage your reviewer to use a specific format, I suggest you do the following. Review this chapter and the following two on reviewing published literature and expanding and revising literature reviews to decide what information and organizational process would best help you consider the quality and revision of your own literature review.

If you're going to do a peer critique of someone else's work, the following information can help you maximize your assistance to others (or to yourself).

Literature Reviews Made Easy, pages 125–129
Copyright © 2010 by Information Age Publishing
All rights of reproduction in any form reserved.
125

Why do a peer critique or simulate a peer critique? Peer critiques give you a chance to learn by:

1. Examining someone else's work (or your own work) to review effectiveness.
2. Reflecting on your own work based on what you've learned while conducting critiques.
3. Develop a plan to improve your own work based on your new insights.

You can learn from a peer critique even if you don't have a chance to conduct a critique of someone else's literature review. You can do a critique of your own literature review, although you need to practice objectivity. One of the purposes of having someone else do your critique is to gain the benefit of objectivity. Because you're close to your work, you may be unaware of pieces of your logic pattern or your argument presentation that are ineffective or are missing. This will be a challenge that you will need to keep in mind as you read, but is one that you can conquer.

In addition, or as an alternative, you can conduct a review of published literature reviews. This gives you the chance to review similar types of literature reviews—simple, applied, or academic. Suggestions for that type of review are included in the following.

Why are there so many different methods of conducting critiques of literature reviews (COLR)? Not everyone benefits from the same information. The outline form in this chapter, suggested for COLR, provides the person whose work is being reviewed with information on strengths and weaknesses in outline form, which can help that person make changes more effectively. The format used for COLR on published works allows the reviewer to examine a literature review that's been successfully completed to identify methods that work.

Peer review of your own work. Before going any farther, though, consider for a moment how you can do a peer review on your own work. Often, writers become so familiar with their writing that they can't review, edit, or proof their own material well. How can you break through that familiarity wall that will interfere with your ability to identify your problems? The answer can be simple.

How much time do you have to complete your literature review? It will be possible for you to do your own peer reviewing relatively objectively if you can do several things:

1. Give yourself a break of two weeks or more before shifting from writing your materials to reviewing them. If you wish to continue working during that time, you can do your reviewing in sections. Work on one section as you review another. That will give you time to allow for a needed break from your work so you can see it more objectively.
2. Read the literature review when you have time to pay close attention to what you're reading. Remember, this is not a simple read for interest. It's a detailed, in-depth read for methods, content, and logic.
3. As you read, develop the COLR suggested in this section.
4. Try to complete your reading and COLR of the literature review, or of the selected section of your review, in one sitting. Doing that will give you the best chance to read into your paper only what's there, as well as to not lose the flow of your review so you can identify where your material is not easily read and quickly understood by the average reader.
5. If you're doing a COLR of your own paper, don't try to read it all at the same time. Compressing your read can cause you to skim rather than read details and will reinforce a natural tendency to miss gaps in logic or presentation. Read about 20 pages at the most at a time so that you stay fresh and attentive.

To do a COLR of a literature review, either someone else's or your own, you can read the draft and complete an outline of the points made by the writer and the authors the writer chose to cite. Finally, you can answer the following questions about each article used to support a particular point.

1. Was that article choice appropriate?
2. Did the article share the information the author indicated was intended?
3. Was the information about the article written concisely so that no extra words, particularly extra prepositional phrases, are used?
4. Was the information integrated well so that the presentation is logical and easy to follow?
5. Was the point the writer was trying to make made effectively?

This is an example of what a peer review outline might look like:

1. Introduction
   a. Topic question—What impact, if any, would a Fortune 500 management training program have on teachers' management effectiveness within their classrooms?
   b. Topic subquestions examined here—
      i. What is known about the role of teachers as managers?
      ii. What similarities and differences exist between teachers as managers and Fortune 500 business mid-level managers?
      iii. What training occurs currently for teachers as classroom managers?
      iv. How effective is the training currently occurring for teachers as classroom managers?
      v. What similarities and differences exist between teacher training programs and Fortune 500 business mid-level manager training programs?
   a. Why important—
      i. Currently, breakdown in classroom management—James (2004)—effective; Irving (2001)—acceptable, but weaker
      ii. Breakdown in classroom management affects education, safety in classroom—James (2004)—connection not made well; Irving (2004)—weak
2. A Comparison of Roles
   a. Discussion of nature of teacher
      i. Smith (1925, p. 23)—teacher caregiver
         1. Smith considers only younger ages, not older
         2. Smith interview sample small
      ii. Jones (2000, p. 25)—"a teacher is perceptive and interceptive"
         1. Doesn't reinforce Smith, but doesn't contradict
         2. Interviews with teachers of students at different ages
      iii. Examination points
         1. Two aren't same, but fit together—point successful
         2. Teachers' perceptions of their roles is important—author observation, point successful
         3. Teachers' target groups affect their perceptions of roles—author observation, evidence not well connected

Practice

Develop critiques of others' literature reviews, and then develop a critique of your own.

Discussion or Writing Activity

Review the narrative of your literature review. Rewrite the literature review narrative. Make it no more than 250 words. This can serve both as an abstract for your literature review and as a clarification of your final literature review that will allow you to discuss it with others.

24

Reviewing Completed Publications

Why conduct a review of a previously completed publication that contains a literature review? How can you benefit from it? You can see how a final literature review looks. You can see how it's structured and how it's phrased. You can examine similarities and differences between both the content and format of your literature review. You can identify areas you'll want to examine and revise in your own work.

There are numerous forms that could be developed to critique completed literature reviews and publications. One that's useful was provided in the previous chapter on peer critiquing. It supports an examination of both overall and detailed goals and the logic presented in the literature review. Another is in the following chapter. The first—in the previous chapter— gives you a chance to examine the flow of the literature review, while the second—in the following chapter—allows you to examine the effectiveness of specific points more closely. Both are useful frameworks.

Were you ever a debater? If you were, you've seen the flow sheets debaters create. It's what an outline can give to you that a simple list of questions cannot. You literally chronicle each point being made, the nature and qual-

Literature Reviews Made Easy, pages 131–134
Copyright © 2010 by Information Age Publishing
All rights of reproduction in any form reserved.

ity of the evidence presented, and whether or not that point falls to your opponents' side or your side. (For techniques that help debaters *flow* debates better that may also help you plan your review better, visit the following site to get information on debating: http://debate.uvm.edu/NFL/rostrumlib/ CheshierNov00.pdf .

Based on the information shared on that site, here are some questions to ask and some procedures that will help you in your review:

1. Practice outlining and reviewing every chance you get. If you read a peer-reviewed article or someone else's literature review from a dissertation proposal or grant application, practice critiquing it to see how the literature reviews are strong or weak and, where strong, how they're worded or organized.

2. Pay close attention to overviews—do they include everything they need to allow a strong logic flow? What techniques do the authors' use to make them strong and to present the information interestingly and effectively?

3. Give yourself space to create your outline and critique. Perhaps you'll find a modified clustering organization a better way to review a given literature review.

4. Pay attention to the citations and the quality of the sources. Are peer-reviewed articles or unbiased sources and local sources used appropriately? Based on the quality of the sources and what they say, are the conclusions drawn by the author appropriate?

5. As you flow, make sure you put in enough details about the literature review to let you return to your evaluation later. Otherwise, you'll be unable to glean any information from it that will help you with your own literature review. Speaking from experience, short notes about something that makes a strong impression on you at one point may not mean much a month later after you've read a number of other pieces.

6. Make sure that you write legibly and that you stick closely to whatever organizational design you use for your critique. As you progress, depending on the length of the literature review you are yourself critiquing, it can become easy to lose track of your organizational form or the organizational level you are reading at the moment.

7. As much as possible, put the information you write into your own words. It will both ring truer to you and will prevent you from inadvertently plagiarizing anywhere in your literature review process.

8. After you've completed your critique of the literature review, give yourself a day or so away from it. When you've gotten some distance from the work, go back to your review. Does it have everything you need? Do you have any questions about what you read or what you wrote?

Remember, when you critique a completed literature review, your goal is to determine whether the logic is effective, whether the documents used support the arguments presented, and whether the conclusions are valid. To do that, you must often follow each step of the logic and documentation path, as the format above indicates.

Errors don't occur in the large, obvious brush strokes of most paintings. Neither are errors in literature reviews normally easily identified by examining the large arguments that are constructed with the series of smaller arguments. Since they normally occur in the small, less-than-obvious details, your job is to find those less-than-obvious issues in a literature review. You may be sure those conclusions are errors, if they exist. What's your goal? It is to guarantee that, before accepting the conclusions presented in any literature review, you're sure those conclusions are based on accurate information that has been interpreted correctly.

As you review this and all future literature, remember the six higher order thinking skills, remember your article analysis process, and consider creating an outline to see how effective and accurate the discussion of literature is.

Practice

Read and critique several literature reviews. Practice putting in as much detail as useful in your critique. Determine whether arguments are presented logically. Are there any pieces missing? Is the logic path direct and clear? Use the peer critique questions as guidelines.

Discussion or Writing Activity

Develop written narratives of the strengths, weaknesses, conclusions, and relative value of each of the published literature reviews and articles you examined. Make your discussions of each literature review and article no more than 500 words, and describe the quality of the work included, the major points and conclusions, and their importance to creating research or change projects of some type.

Other Resources

http://www.utoronto.ca/hswriting/lit-review.htm

25

Expanding and Revising

Expanding a literature review and revising it are part of a conscious plan to improve its quality. This expansion and revision plan can be developed after either receiving a peer critique of your literature review draft or after conducting your own self-critique of your literature review. This process gives you a chance to evaluate the effectiveness of your writing; identify areas that need to be strengthened, trimmed, or eliminated; and consider what steps to take to correct any identified issues.

To help you with this process, some questions are presented below. Either you or your peer can answer these questions using the perspective of an evaluator or editor rather than of the writer. By doing that, you can create some distance from the words and ideas you've written. Since people can experience the same attachment to and sense of protectiveness about their work as a woman when she gives birth, developing that distance is essential to honestly evaluating your work.

Since the questions are framed to create as much objectivity as possible, answer the questions as they are phrased. These questions can provide the basis of your plan to expand and revise your literature review.

Literature Reviews Made Easy, pages 135–137
Copyright © 2010 by Information Age Publishing
All rights of reproduction in any form reserved.   **135**

1. Was the initial question you used clearly or unclearly stated? If you have more than one initial question, which of them were clearly or unclearly stated?
2. Which of your initial questions were well supported by logic and evidence and which needed extra logical and evidentiary support?
3. Which of your subquestions were logically organized to allow sequential consideration of the issues involved and which needed to be reorganized or strengthened?
4. Which of your subquestions were clearly and unclearly stated?
5. Which of your subquestions were supported with adequate research evidence and which needed extra research evidence?
   a. Were there any assumptions made in the logical presentation of information that might make the argument weaker?
      i. Can the argument be tightened up with other literature?
      ii. Do any of the comments that were not conditional need to be made conditional (potential concerns or observations rather than statements)?
      iii. Does this part of the argument need to be dropped?
   b. Were there any limitations to any evidence used in subquestion arguments?
      i. Does an article look at a group unlike the group being examined in the literature review as a whole or a group with limited similarity to the group being examined?
      ii. Does an article cover unique or unusual periods of time or events that limit its ability to help with overall subquestion or argument considerations?
   c. Was the evidence used correctly interpreted?
6. Were the conclusions logical?
   a. Were they based on a systematic, realistic examination of the data?
   b. Were they appropriate to the types of studies and data provided in the articles used?
   c. Did they integrate all of the data, or were they biased?
   d. Were they presented logically?
7. Were the conclusions clear?
   a. Was the relationship between the questions and conclusions clearly stated?
   b. Was the relationship between the questions and conclusions logically presented?
   c. Were the conclusions appropriate to the questions and the data?

8. Were the conclusions linked effectively to the initial questions and subquestions?
   a. Were the questions restated, either directly or indirectly?
   b. Was the link between the questions and conclusions stated clearly?
   c. Was the link between the questions and conclusions linked to the importance of the questions and conclusions? In other words, did the "so what" question get answered?

Once you've completed this series of questions, consider what that means to your literature review. What changes do you need to make?

One way to plan your next step is to return to the answers you've provided. Note in the answers what you need to alter, and make a plan to develop those alterations. What do you need to augment with additional research? What do you need to cut? What plan will you use to make your improvements?

Practice

Conduct a practice peer review on Chapter 2 (Literature Review) of at least two dissertations using the questions and outline above. Following that, conduct a self-review of your own literature review.

Discussion and Writing Activity

Draft an outline of changes you wish to make to your literature review based on your self-review. In addition, rewrite pieces of information you identify as needing improvement.

26

Structuring Your Work

As discussed earlier, the organization you use as you present analyses, comparisons, contrasts, evaluations, syntheses, and integrations does not have to be set in stone. What does matter, though, is that readers can follow your logic. So, here are some important facts for planning your presentation:

1. Is your analysis clearly linked to the article you're analyzing?
2. Have you clearly presented which articles you're comparing and which you're contrasting?
3. Can the reader tell when you're shifting to evaluating the literature against your topic, question, or circumstance? Do you introduce this shift to clarify the strengths and weaknesses of the articles?
4. Can readers tell when you shift to and from your own assessments and the assessments and conclusions of the authors you examine, as well as when you shift to evaluating against your topic, question, or circumstance?
5. Do you use your synthesis and integration as a capstone, or culmination of your research, before your conclusion to help you and your readers see what does or does not fit into the overall picture?

Literature Reviews Made Easy, pages 139–142
Copyright © 2010 by Information Age Publishing
All rights of reproduction in any form reserved.   **139**

Much of your decision about organization will be based on whether you structure your review around researchers or around topics. If you review researchers—researcher 1, researcher 2, researcher 3, and so on—then your article summary and analysis will often be separate from your analysis and be presented first before your other examinations or assessments. If you review topics—the price of tea in China, the price of tea in India, the price of tea in Europe, and what that means to the price of tea in the United States—then your article summaries, analyses, and comparisons and contrasts will often be combined under your topic headings. Your synthesis and integration will virtually always come separately just prior to your conclusions, regardless of what type of organizational design you use.

How can you identify what structure will work best for you? First, consider your question. Second, examine your research. Is the information you're gleaning from the articles addressing your subject clustered around theorists. Or is it clustered around events, dimensions of a topic, or another topic-related characteristic? Determining which organizational structure to use for your literature review doesn't have to be complicated. Often the research itself will help you identify what structure would be best to use.

So, as you consider how to structure your literature review, it's helpful to review your outline. Consider what you're discovering in your literature. What are your main points? Are they sorting themselves around theorists, events, or specific situations? Possibly, there's no clear direction in which the information is sorting itself. If that's the case, then any structure is as good as another. However, if there is an organizational structure suggested, it would be best to use that structure.

As a final step, consider the logic presented in your review by drawing an if–then diagram. Figure 26.1 is an example of an if–then diagram.

This is obviously not your standard if–then chart. There's a reason for that. After several attempts to make a traditional if-then chart work, it became obvious that the multiple cause environment experienced most often in literature reviews was not conducive to creating a traditional if-then diagram. So, this cluster-style if–then diagram was developed instead.

As you can see on the diagram, direct if-then links have been created. Since there can be no direct causal relationship identified and literature reviews are meant to be objective considerations of multiple perspectives, multiple if-then possibilities are identified.

When you examine this chart closely, you'll notice that abuse and neglect are listed as *then* items for family and no-family trauma issues. As you develop your literature review, considering whether traumas occurred within the family or outside the family becomes important because of the possible

If-Then Diagram

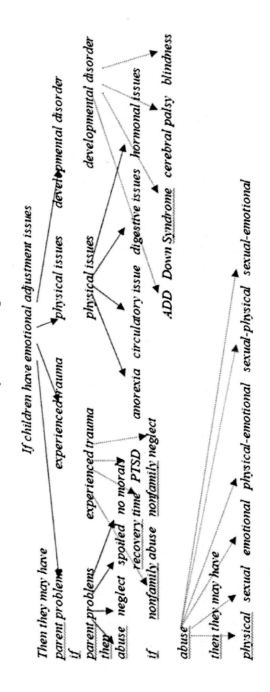

Figure 26.1 If–then diagram.

differences in impact abuse from those two sources might produce. It is also important to mention each step so that no steps in the correlational links are missed. So, as you draw your if–then chart, you need to consider whether you have documented and expressed every link on the if-then chart.

Practice

Examine your review. How have you structured your paper? Review past materials on organization. Do one final review here of how you've organized your review using the above final criteria. Then, when that's done, sit down and draw an if–then diagram for every logic link you're presenting in your literature review.

Discussion and Writing Activity

Restructure any portions of your transitional materials required. Make sure that your logic lines, connections between ideas, and other relevant structural points are effective.

27

Formulating Introductions

Formulating strong introductions that catch readers' attention is the first step in making interesting. Catching the readers' attention in the first few minutes can make a great difference.

Introductions don't have to be dry statements of interest in a topic. Here are a few ideas you can use when thinking of how to plan your introduction.

1. What was it that got you interested in the topic? Can you share that in your introduction to get the readers' attention?
2. What is the main point of the theoretical framework you've developed from your literature review? Can you use it as the main point at the beginning of your introduction?
3. What is the importance of your review? What "so what?" answer does it help you address? Can you share that to get your readers' interest?

As you consider these questions, remember that your literature review's introduction should discuss your topic in the initial paragraph. It doesn't

Literature Reviews Made Easy, pages 143–147
Copyright © 2010 by Information Age Publishing
All rights of reproduction in any form reserved.

have to say, "This is my topic." It should somehow describe, consider, or discuss it, though. Why? The reader should be able to understand at least what your topic is going to be as the paper begins.

Remember, too, that a paragraph is made up of a topic sentence, sentences that describe and explain your topic sentence by giving greater detail, and a sentence that leads into the next paragraph or next topic. Why is this important? This paragraph structure lets your reader understand quickly and explicitly what you're examining. It also makes your work *flow* so that you don't lose your readers with complicated sentence and paragraph structure before you begin to share your literature review.

Your introduction should begin with your basic topic, explain why it's important, and describe what your perspective or interest is. Then it should segue into the review of literature.

In addition to using the information provided here, read the introductions to a number of peer-reviewed articles and dissertation literature reviews. This will give you a greater understanding of the variety of ways introductions are constructed.

Meanwhile, here are a couple of introductions to help you get an idea of how to formulate an introduction.

Introduction 1:

Unlike many classrooms utilizing autocratic management methods, democratic classrooms have been shown to both alter students' perceptions of their classroom experiences and shift the teacher out of the position of class autocrat and into the position of class facilitator. As early as 1993, Schechtman determined that students in democratic classrooms developed greater senses of belonging and of freedom to express their feelings, as well as greater opportunities for sharing. As a result, social attitude-impacting democratic programs are often used in social studies classrooms where democratically constructed classroom interactions and behavioral expectations foster positive interactions and greater understanding of different cultural groups (Davis, 2007). In such programs, students develop more open communications and stronger beliefs that social justice rather than arbitrariness are preferable. They demonstrated more responsible behavior in other classes. They also demonstrated greater respect for themselves and others both inside and outside the classroom. Taken to the school level, researchers and theorists have developed school models like the Just Community Model, the Lab School, or the Children's Republic (Engel, 2008; Tappan, 1998).

However, although student attitudes and understanding can be enhanced through participation in democratic programs, most schools are unable to fully integrate democratic educational methods throughout the school. In addition, student attitude and student failure are impacted by a number of other factors that can at least in part ameliorate the impact of democratic education. Students lacking the family support needed to succeed in traditional schools, for example, are more prone to negative self-esteem, lack of school completion, and later delinquency and life failures (Adams & Adams, 1996; Beman, 1995; Bynum & Dunn, 1996; Caspi, Henry, Moffitt & Silva, 1996; McCabe, 1997; Pabon, Rodriguez, & Gurin, 1992; Roizblatt et al., 1997; Sheets, Sandler, & West, 1996; Winters, 1997). Previous school experiences, including bullying, parental relationships, having a parent who did not complete high school, being from a single parent family in early childhood, suspensions, low socioeconomic status, low grade point averages, and having repeated a grade also predispose students to academic challenges and failure (Englund, Egeland, & Collins, 2008; Pagani et al., 2008; Suhyun Su, Jingyo Su, & Houston, 2007; Townsend, Flisher, Chikobvu, Lombard, & King, 2008).

The desire to work or personal factors that create the need for employment also can place a strain on already at risk students' schedules, negatively impacting their academic success (Lee & Staff, 2007; Warren & Cataldi, 2006). At the same time, students who drop out of school can experience subsequent success in employment and higher education if able to complete their high school education later, but often as GED graduates still experience less success in the areas of income, life satisfaction, future optimism, symptoms of severe depression, and substance use than high school graduates. (Suh-Ruu O, 2008; Vanttaja & Jarvinen, 2006). (Dawidowicz, 2008, pp. 1–2)

Notice that the article introduces the concept of democratic classrooms having an impact on students' attitudes. It describes an educational community model. Finally, it introduces the fact that a specific school is being examined, including the school's purpose, and that the study of that school is going to evaluate the effectiveness of democratic classrooms for changing students' attitudes.

Introduction 2:

During adolescence, students accomplish the final stages of self-definition that carry them into adulthood. Students test their personalities and behaviors in various situations against the expectations and reactions of others. As others respond to their behaviors and choices, adolescents redefine and hone their actions and reactions enough to form behavior episodes that stabilize their personalities. This period of growth and self-definition proves extremely important in preventing the emotional traumas adults experience when they have missed this stage and must define themselves by growing through normally adolescent developmental stages during adulthood (Ho, Lempers & Clark-Lempers, 1995; Field, Lang, Yando & Bendell, 1995; Liu, Kaplan & Risser, 1992; Pabon, Rodriguez & Gurin, 1992; Ford, 1992).

However, by its very nature, cyber distance learning negates the opportunity for participating adolescents' to fulfill those socialization growth needs by eliminating the regular interaction they experience during traditional high school attendance. However, how Utah has provided that learning experience while utilizing a cyber high school demonstrates a model for other states interested in developing a program providing the "best of both learning worlds." (Dawidowicz, 2000, p. 2)

Notice that this author jumps right into the topic. However, the author doesn't say, "This is what I'm studying." Instead, the author begins to explain the nature of the problem and to introduce the interests to be considered in the literature review.

Introduction 3:

The cold March wind cut through the coats of the members of the Continental Congress as they ratified the Bill of Rights in New York City in 1789, but the fire that burned in their hearts kept out the chill. That fire burned for the rights they had just guaranteed their families and their descendants, the first of which was the right to the free practice of religion. (Dawidowicz, 2001, p. 1)

Notice that this introduction is literary. It is the introduction to a dissertation as a whole, not to the Chapter 2 literature review. You can use a literary introduction, as long as it's brief and acceptable to your consumer—your chair, committee, or supervisor. However, this type of introduction is normally used for a dissertation or larger piece of literature than a literature review. The introduction for the literature review of this particular dissertation looked like this.

No direct research exists on the evolution within Utah of either the education systems or students as a result of the increasingly heterogeneous environment. Therefore, this literature review covers materials that lay the groundwork for understanding and assessing educational environment changes and students' behavioral changes in Utah's newly hydrogenised and hydrogenising high schools. Since Utah is in the process of cultural diversification, each formative factor will be addressed as it occurs both within the country at large and within Utah's unique traditional culture. (Dawidowicz, 2001, p. 19)

In other words, whether you're writing an introduction for the literature review of a dissertation, an article, or a study, you're going to write a simple, direct introduction. However, if you're creating an introduction for a larger piece and wish to create interest in your topic before you begin your literature review, you can create a longer, more detailed introduction.

Practice

Review the information provided in this section. Consider your literature review topic, as well as the topic of your larger document if your literature review is part of a larger piece.

Consider what points would be important to share in the introduction. Draft an introduction for your literature review. In addition, if your literature review is part of a larger essay, create an introduction for that piece, as well.

Discussion or Writing Activity

Review your introduction. Consider whether it shares the information you should use to introduce your topic. Does it share your passion about the topic? Does it share enough information to lay a strong groundwork for your reader? Rewrite it as appropriate.

References

Dawidowicz, P. (2008). *"The Beginning of a Solution": School Design, Self-Efficacy, Completion Rates, and Creation of Community.* Bloomington, IN: Creative Visions in Education Group (CreaVEGroup). Retrieved from the ERIC database. (ED501747)

Dawidowicz, P. (2001). *"Sometimes you gotta learn the concept, not just the rules": Educational and cultural impacts of Utah's diversification process.* Ann Arbor, MI: UMI Press.

Dawidowicz, P. (2000). *Addressing adolescent needs for socialization in the distance learning environment.* Springfield, MA: Center for Successful Communities. Retrieved from the ERIC database. (ED508997)

28

Formulating Conclusions

What make strong conclusions that summarize exactly what you want to share? Regardless of the type of literature review you're writing, a conclusion should restate:

1. Your topic or question.
2. The reason your topic or question is important.
3. The main points your critique of research revealed.
4. Your conclusions.
5. What it means to your next step—your research study, your design, your grant—or your, "so what?"

Here are some examples.

Conclusion 1:

These data indicate wide-ranging applications. Perhaps most important is the nature of a religion-based society itself. Data indicated that moral education in such a society is passive, normally left to parents, but that notable

Literature Reviews Made Easy, pages 149–153
Copyright © 2010 by Information Age Publishing
All rights of reproduction in any form reserved.

149

numbers of parents may for whatever reason surrender that right and responsibility to others without concern for the quality or nature of education received by their children. Others might simply neglect to fulfill their moral education responsibility.

This study suggests further, that the distinction between living one's culture and living one's religion may merit further investigation. Certainly, the pregnancy rate in the undiversified area raises the question of whether religion as culture becomes a less binding and effective moral compass or, perhaps, a totally ineffective moral binding or compass. It also indicates further investigation into the effectiveness of having a state institution mandate localities' moral education policies and procedures would prove useful, since those programs' effectiveness are reliant upon the dedication and follow-through of local teachers and administrators.

It also raises the question of whether or not changes or challenges from outside a culture should be considered, at least in some cases, worth the potential negative effects. As a result of immigrant influxes, state residents raised their expectations for honesty and acceptable behavior from individuals in office and public servants. In diversified and diversifying areas, parents and public officials reaffirmed their rights and responsibilities to participate in their children's positive enculturation. The question continues to be whether the potential positive effects outweigh the potential negative effects. Such reactions as gang formation were negative. However, the galvanizing effect of challenges to belief systems and reaffirmation of goals also evidenced in diversified areas among teachers and students also indicates that challenge to acculturated religion can also be positive.

Given the increasing diversification of state and world populations, these questions merit further investigation. Certainly, Utah's culture will continue to change. As the state becomes more diversified, researchers will undoubtedly examine through extensive studies both the short-and long-term to verify whether adolescents' exposure to multiple moral choices, based on their parents' traditional LDS standards, will corrupt them. To determine the reality in Utah will require further study. (Dawidowicz, 2003, pp. 288–289)

Note that at the point where a conclusion is created, there are no citations. This is a place for summary and driving home the points evolved in the literature review. Notice, further, that this conclusion also includes a description of the types of future research that should also be done. This is something you may also find relevant as you develop your literature review. What was on your cluster diagram for which you could find no research? What was on your cluster diagram that you didn't explore that would be important to consider in future research?

Conclusion 2:

Since this study explores changes in behaviors that develop as a result of a number of factors, it proves important to understand how both variations in and the interactions of these factors can further exacerbate already potentially difficult situations. Inadequate and insensitive educational facilities and personnel, population shifts, single-parent families, low socio-economic status, negative peer influences, inadequate character education within the home, and lack of student acceptance of responsibility number among such combining factors. These factors will be examined briefly to create an understanding of the potential effects of these factors that will allow at least partial contextualization of study results. Although no causal or quantifiable correlative relationships will be identified, this data will allow effective consideration of future potential clarifying research questions.

In Utah, by both federal and state law no information is either available or can be gathered within the schools on the numbers of single-parent families, the nature of activities within the home, individuals' religions, or individuals' moral or activity choices without special approval. Therefore, information will not be gathered from students themselves, but through others' observations of students' activities and educational systems' changes.

However, as data is gathered from individuals to be interviewed, some insight into whether school staffs' are either inadequate and insensitive or adequate and sensitive. Although this information may be identified, it will not be the focus of this study except as it pertains to the evolution of Utah's educational system as a result of the cultural diversification process. It will, however, allow researchers to begin to draw a picture of what life within Utah's new multicultural schools is like that will prove useful in future studies.

Impact on Research Design

Information gathered during the literature review indicated that recent Utah laws forbid individuals from gathering information within the schools on the numbers of single-parent families, the nature of activities within the home, individuals' religions, or individuals' moral or activity choices without special approval, and little if any information existed from state-acceptable research sources. Therefore, information was not gathered from students themselves, but through interviews with adults who had observed students' activities and educational systems' changes.

Further, due to the inability to enter any schools other than the Horizontal School and the Alpine Life and learning Center for the purposes of observation, direct student observations could not be conducted. Therefore, it proved impossible to observe both student-teacher and student-student interactions directly.

. . .

The inability to conduct direct observations precluded the examination of all facets of student communication, conflict, and moral behaviors. Therefore, for the purposes of this study, communication behaviors examined did not include nonverbal behaviors or ethnic-specific expression differences and shifts. Instead, it included indications of language shift, particularly to the use of profanity or hate language directed at any group. It also included evidence of effective or ineffective communication as indicated in various reported sources and interviews. Conflict behaviors examined included violent and argumentative incidents, examined both for numbers of occurrences and for whether they were hate-oriented. Finally, moral behaviors examined encompassed a wider range of activities due to the nature of the LDS culture. They included sexual activity acceptability and orientation shifts, changes in standards of language and honest, shifts in respect levels and dress standards, and more. (Dawidowicz, 2001, pp. 86–88)

This conclusion is from a dissertation proposal. Notice that it includes not just a consideration of all factors, but also a consideration of how the data gathered and conclusions drawn impact the research design itself. That is a part of the conclusion to a literature review.

Conclusion 3:

The traditional smokestack school paradigm considers technology a teacher, while the modern information technology paradigm sees technology rather as a resource and facilitator. Although EHS students' long-term activities, educational successes, and life adjustment have yet to be examined and students' opportunities to learn cooperative and collaborative interactions have yet to be addressed, the program offers numerous advantages. They include lowered costs for schools and parents, flexible schedules, quality education, opportunities for accelerated learning, and more.

As episodes like Littleton illustrate, one important advantage is that, even in the cyber environment, its emphasis on human interaction and adolescent socialization continues to exist. Although many see technology as the needed panacea to cure all evils—allowing cost cutting, compensating for local physical or personnel resource shortages, and allowing the student to control the speed of educational advancement—society cannot afford to forget the need to provide positive social interaction. Utah's EHS provides both positive cyber opportunities and the opportunity for maintained IRL opportunities that gives its students, perhaps, the best of both worlds. (Dawidowicz, 2002, p. 73)

This conclusion is straightforward, points out strengths and weaknesses of the research, and highlights the limitations of the literature.

Practice

Review the information provided in this section. Read a number of peer-reviewed article and literature review conclusions. Review your literature review, and identify the important points made in your literature review. Then draft a conclusion for your literature review.

Discussion or Writing Activity

Review your conclusion. Consider whether it shares the information you should share to summarize your topic. Does it share your most important points? Does it share enough information to inform your reader of your work's importance? Does it lay the groundwork for either your research design or your change project? Rewrite it as appropriate.

References

Dawidowicz, P. (2003). Teaching morality in schools in Utah's religion-based society. *Journal of Moral Education, 32*(3), 275–289.

Dawidowicz, P. (2001). *"Sometimes you gotta learn the concept, not just the rules": Educational and cultural impacts of Utah's diversification process.* Ann Arbor, MI: UMI Press.

Dawidowicz, P. (2000). *Addressing adolescent needs for socialization in the distance learning environment.* Springfield, MA: Center for Successful Communities. Retrieved from the ERIC database. (ED508997)

29

Revisions and Editing

You've completed a peer review of your literature review. You've considered what needs to be strengthened, rewritten, or removed. You've written your introduction and conclusion. What needs to be done before your literature review can be finalized?

Before finalizing your literature review, you'll need to use the editing process. Editing is examining your work with several questions in mind.

1. Are your sentences clear?
2. Are possessives and plurals written correctly?
3. Are titles and names all correct?
4. Is grammar throughout correct?
5. Is spelling correct?
6. Are sentences worded as simply and directly as possible?
   a. Is active rather than passive tense used as much as possible?
   b. Are colloquial terms not used?
   c. Are there no extra prepositional phrases?
7. Is punctuation correct?

Literature Reviews Made Easy, pages 155–157
Copyright © 2010 by Information Age Publishing
All rights of reproduction in any form reserved.

8. Are lists presented correctly in paragraphs or as separate lists?
9. Are citations presented for all paraphrasing?
10. Are quotation marks and citations used for all quotations?
11. Are references present and formed correctly?

In other words, is everything presented correctly from a technical standpoint?

Review this list of questions. Then review your work. If in doubt about the strength of your writing, you can hire an editor. However, before considering that, start by using Microsoft Word's spelling and grammar check. It will not identify all of your writing's issues, but it will identify enough to give you a good start.

As you use this Microsoft's Word program and the list above, you will benefit from personalizing the list. As you identify specific words you tend to misspell, specific phrases you tend to use incorrectly, or other regular problems with your writing, add an entry to the list to remind you to check for that problem in all future writing.

Good grammar and attention to detail make the difference between your work looking polished and you looking conscientious instead of your work looking slipshod and you looking sloppy and unconcerned about developing quality work. It is worth taking the time to do a good job.

Practice

Review your material using the checklist just provided. Correct any errors you identify. If you have questions about anything, use the APA manual and the websites listed at the end of this chapter to get answers to your potential questions.

Discussion or Writing Activity

Review your literature review with a reader's eye. Consider whether your sentences alternate between long and short, that you use literature with the right amount of technical wording, and that you write in a style appropriate to the type of review you are creating. Rewrite any material required to finalize your literature review.

Other Resources

http://grammar.ccc.commnet.edu/grammar
http://owl.english.purdue.edu/handouts/grammar/index.html

http://owl.english.purdue.edu/handouts/research/index.html
http://www.ucalgary.ca/UofC/eduweb/grammar/
http://www.refdesk.com/factgram.html
http://www.apastyle.org/elecref.html

30

Summary of the Writing Process

When we refer to the writing process, it's important to remember that we need to use several processes almost religiously to ensure that not just a strong review of the literature is created, but also a strong written product. Those stages are planning, researching (which has been covered only slightly here), organizing, drafting, reviewing, revising, reviewing, revising, and editing. Notice that there is reviewing, revising, reviewing, and more revising.

The implication here is that you should cycle through the reviewing, revising, and editing process at least twice for a product as large as a literature review. Why? Remember, a literature review is a living organism. It evolves as a child does through the research, writes, and rewrites you develop. You, as the investigator, gather new clues with each piece of information you read and incorporate into your critical thinking assessment.

To maximize your success at each individual stage, remember that you need to use a strong organizational process. You will be using varying amounts of information based on the type of literature review you're creating, but all will require a good organizational method. The use of brain-

Literature Reviews Made Easy, pages 159–163
Copyright © 2010 by Information Age Publishing
All rights of reproduction in any form reserved.
159

storming clustering, outlining, and the forms provided in this book will allow you to maintain strong organization.

Outlining also serves another purpose. As your knowledge of the information you want to place in your literature review evolves, update your outline. Accordingly, you can identify where in your literature review draft you can insert the newly acquired information. Remember that, although there are distinct stages of the writing process, and although before writing can begin a certain amount of research must occur, it is normal for people to be writing their literature reviews while still conducting research.

That said, each stage in the writing development process has a distinct purpose. Planning occurs after you've developed your question, done a preliminary survey of the literature available on your topic, and identified your questions. It is the process of conducting your free writing and clustering activities and planning your outline based on the literature you found available on your topic in your initial survey of the literature. Remember that your literature review by definition is an objective evaluation of your topic and situation. That means, as you develop and evolve your cluster and outline, you need to build into those activities an unbiased, objective consideration of your topic.

Your research gathering process can begin as you're doing your planning, or it can begin shortly after the planning stage. Either way, it will continue throughout most of your literature review writing process. One of your first research activities, though, will coincide with your planning activities. You will develop a preliminary determination of which articles you're going to review. However, you need to remember you're not locked into these articles. They are preliminary, and you may determine some don't contain information you can use. So, as you progress, continue to review and evaluate articles that may or may not be useful to you. The organizing phase can include a number of activities. It occurs after you've done some research and have a greater understanding of the articles you want to integrate into your outline and your research. It might include the revision of your outline, but it always includes the organization of your literature to identify which articles you can use to support which perspectives or points on your outline.

Drafting is the process of writing, which can begin as soon as you begin generating ideas. Normally, drafting is an ongoing process. Even the most prolific writers rarely write a product as large as a literature review in one or two sittings. Often, the process of writing itself helps people to see more clearly how the pieces of that review fit together and which points they want to share. In addition, they also help to smooth out logic connection issues that may not become obvious in the clustering, initial outlining, and ongoing outlining process.

Reviewing occurs periodically when you determine you need to conduct a review. The reasons for conducting a review is to ensure you're following your plan and your outline, to ensure that your logic makes sense, and to ensure that your wording is as professional and effective as you would like it to be.

Reviewing is most easily accomplished by taking a few days' break after writing a draft so that you have time to get a distance from the exact wording, phrasing, and thoughts you planned to write. Often, as people write, they will complete in their minds thoughts they only partially commit to paper. Taking a break gives you time to become less familiar with the words you've written so that you can more easily recognize the holes and ineffective passages that exist in that writing.

Remember to use the outlining technique for what you've written to see whether your points are made effectively. Revising is the improvement of whatever is weak, so whatever you identify as needing revision you should rewrite until you feel it is effective.

Finally, after reviewing and revising at least two times, you reach the editing stage. Editing is examining the material for directness, proper format and grammar, and correct APA usage, if it's an academic literature review in education or the social sciences. Remember that, even though your formatting requirements will be slightly different for a simple literature review or an applied literature review, your grammar and directness standards will still be the same.

Notice that the discussion of conducting a review of your literature review was placed near the end of this description of the writing process. However, a literature review, like any written product, is a living organism while it's being written. Pausing halfway through the production process to review the direction that your research and writing have taken allows you an opportunity to consider whether your work is staying on track. Remember, literature reviews often deal with potentially unwieldy topics. As you conduct your review, you should ask yourself several questions. Is your review of the literature still looking at the same questions? Do you need to alter your questions slightly, make them more specific, or select new questions to make your literature review as strong as possible? Do you need to force yourself to limit the articles you read or review in order to stay on task? Remember, you can always create a file to save those articles that are fascinating but that don't quite fit what you're examining. Later they may fit another review you write.

As you read the articles you review, the forms supplied at the back of this book allow you to organize a systematic critical assessment of the literature used in your review. The forms should help you more easily identify how the literature relates to your topic or questions. They should allow you to shift from article summary to article analysis to critical combination of the literature you've read as you write your literature review.

Those forms are designed to be tailored by you to maximize your success. The form includes categories that may not be useful to you depending on the type of literature review you're developing and the types of articles and literature sources available to you. In addition, depending on your subject, you may need to add some categories not yet entered there. Play with it, and take control of your research process. It is possible to use these forms as printed forms to be filled out by hand, but they are probably better used as template files for a word processing program or as a computer database form. Computerizing the forms makes it easier to organize the articles for your review and also to use the search options of the software you're using to find articles on a particular topic.

Once again, you don't have to present your review in sections such as analysis, comparison and contrast, evaluation, and synthesis and integration. When you organize your reviews by topic instead of author or theorist, you can include analyses, comparisons and contrasts, and evaluations in the discussion as you consider each topic. This more sophisticated organizational pattern systematically examines dimensions of a topic, including multiple perspectives of those dimensions. Organizing by topic means the relationships between different groups of articles on the overall topic and circumstances are presented. That pattern makes it easier for readers to understand and appreciate the information you have identified and the conclusions you have drawn.

Don't forget to include good paragraphs with strong topic sentences that act as umbrellas to the information those paragraphs each share. That means every topic you discuss in the paragraph should be mentioned in some simple manner in the topic sentence. This helps make the paragraph more coherent and focused.

Remember also to use concluding sentences that summarize the information you've shared in the paragraph. Such sentences create a logical segue to the next paragraph by restating the point of that paragraph as strongly as possible. In a well-written literature review, the topic sentences and conclusion sentences would be part of your outline.

Finally, remember that the goal of your work is to objectively explore a question. Is your work objective? Have you considered at least two or three different possibilities about the factors you've identified for your topic? Have you drawn conclusions based not on your experience, but on the weight of the evidence shared in the peer-reviewed articles you read? Have you identified how the research perspectives you've examined either complement or contradict each other and, if they contradict each other, how they can actually complement each other to help create a realistic picture of your topic?

With this review, you have a succinct summary of how to plan, organize, structure, and review your literature review. Remember that this writing process combined with the analysis process to follow will help you succeed in developing a strong literature review.

Other Resources

http://www.ecs.org/html/educationIssues/Research/primer/researchtrustworthy
    .asp
http://www.ecs.org/html/educationIssues/Research/primer/researchwarrants
    .asp

31

Review of Analysis Methods

This is the final section, so it contains a quick review of each of the analysis, or evaluation, methods. Although Bloom's taxonomy identifies critical thinking skills differently, this book presents a simple method of critically evaluating articles. Regardless of the type of literature review you're creating—simple, applied, or academic—you'll use these several steps to help understand the importance to your topic of what you're reading in the sources appropriate to your review.

Analysis

Analysis is the first step in considering any article. It examines the article's accuracy based on sample size and methodology, strength of the research used to draw conclusions, logic behind the research used to draw conclusions, and appropriateness of the conclusions to the research and methodology. It considers the internal integrity of the article and whether it really is valuable as a source within your literature review. Here are the questions once again.

Literature Reviews Made Easy, pages 165–170
Copyright © 2010 by Information Age Publishing
All rights of reproduction in any form reserved.

1. Is the logic behind the study sound? (Does it have a solid theoretical framework?)
   a. Are the literature sources upon which the research design is based sound?
   b. Are they interpreted correctly by the author in the process of laying the ground work for the study?
   c. Is the presentation unbiased, or is it skewed because there is not enough consideration of opposing views and different perspectives on the questions being considered?
2. Is the question being examined sufficiently narrowed and can it be tested accurately?
3. Is the research design appropriate for the question being examined?
   a. If it's a question about a causal relationship, is it an experimental quantitative design or a design like path analysis that allows the researcher to draw causal conclusions?
   b. Is the sample size large enough?
   c. Is it a biased sample?
   d. Is it the wrong type of sample?
   e. Is its methodology examining the specific question being considered?
4. If an article is a not a report of research, are quality resources used in the creation of the article that are treated in an unbiased manner?
   a. Are the sources sufficient and rich enough to support the conclusions drawn?
   b. If the article is exploratory in nature (designed only to consider possibilities and not draw conclusions), does it consider enough possibilities to be unbiased and effective?
5. Do the data as reported appear to have been appropriately interpreted?
6. Are the conclusions that were drawn appropriate for the design and the data collected?
   a. Are the conclusions identified as appropriately limited?
   b. Are the conclusions specific and clear?
7. What are the credentials of the contributors?
   a. Does the author have advanced training and experience in that field of research., or does the author have credentials in the field?
   b. Does the author use quality sources to establish the argument?

Comparison and Contrast

Comparison and contrast are two sides of a coin. These two methods consider how articles are similar to and different from each other. They examine whether articles contradict each other, or reinforce each other, and whether the samples used are different enough to account for the discrepancies or variations in findings. They pave the way for the development of syntheses and integrations later. The questions are supplied once more here.

Comparisons consider:

1. Similarities in theoretical frameworks (logic, research, and rationale behind the position taken and the research question chosen).
2. Similarities in research limitations.
3. Similarities in research assumptions.
4. Similarities in research design.
5. Similarities in research study samples.
6. Similarities in research results.
7. Similarities in research conclusions.

They can be structural (theoretical frameworks, research design, limitations, etc.) or substantive (results or conclusions).

Contrasts consider:

1. Differences in theoretical frameworks (logic, research, and rationale behind the position taken and the research question chosen).
2. Differences in research limitations.
3. Differences in research assumptions.
4. Differences in research design.
5. Differences in research study samples.
6. Differences in research results.
7. Differences in research conclusions.

They also can be structural (theoretical frameworks, research design, limitations, etc.) or substantive (results or conclusions).

Evaluation

Evaluation is the assessment of the literature you are reviewing against a different outside element or factor, normally the topic you're researching in the situation you're examining. In other words, evaluations are often based on an examination of literature against a smaller, more specific topic than the topic being examined. Such topics can include a specific office, classroom, program, or other similar smaller unit or subunit of the overall topic being examined in the literature review.

To maximize an evaluation, you need to consider several factors. These factors help your evaluation—your assessment of what you've learned from the literature in relation to a specific outside topic, circumstance, occurrence, event, or phenomenon—to be both objective and well-linked to the literature you're reviewing.

As you do an evaluation, consider these questions:

1. How well linked is your evaluation point? This link should be close, not distant.
2. How much can it help to evaluate your literature?

    Determine which evaluation point will give you the best chance to understand the literature. How do you do that? Identify which is going to give you different perspectives or insights you can use to compare and contrast programs or factors about your topic that you considered in the literature. There are different facets of each evaluation point to consider. However, the final decision will be based on exactly what is available in the literature.

3. Conduct a comparison of the dynamics explored in the literature to see:
    a. whether there's information on the characteristics of the programs or topics being discussed that you can compare to your topic and situation
    b. whether there's information on a particular issue such as the dynamics of participants' interactions or the chain of command or custody
    c. whether there's information on the emotional support provided by home health care providers that impacts your choice of program to explore

Having done all of this, your goal is to take this information, consider the specific application or environment, examine your goals for the review, and evaluate how the literature reviewed adds to your understanding of your own topic, situation, and environment.

Synthesis and Integration

Developing a synthesis and integration is the process of combining what appear to be complementary and apparently conflicting ideas to create a comprehensive picture of what's happening around your topic and, potentially, in your environment. It's the consideration of all of the information you've gathered to help you gain an understanding about aspects of your topic and your environment so that you can draw conclusions (simple literature review), develop a plan of action or similar product (applied literature review), or develop and justify the importance of a research study (academic literature review).

Syntheses and integrations are opposites of each other, but they function closely together. Syntheses are identified often by commonalities and the ability to explain specific environments. Integrations are identified by their apparent disagreement with syntheses, and they are integrated by identifying their limiting factors and seeing how those limiting factors prevent them from conflicting with the synthesized information.

Here are some guidelines for synthesis:

1. Examine each article's conclusions or major points to see which don't contradict each other. This information will normally come from comparisons you've made, because comparisons by their nature work together instead of contradicting each other.
2. Look at the piece of the overall, "big" picture each of those pieces of information adds.
   a. Put differently, how do these pieces of information weave together to create a spider web, or framework, that will help you understand the environment in which your topic or situation occurs?
   b. How do they reinforce each other?

Before moving on, remember to be careful when creating syntheses. During the process of creating syntheses, researchers are building conclusions based on the linking (or weaving together) of multiple ideas.

This is a point where faulty logic, inappropriately or inaccurately understood or applied information, or overgeneralization can cause fatal errors in the development of a sound literature review. Since a literature review is used to develop a theoretical framework for further research or project development, it's essential to be rigorous in examining literature and data during this synthesis process.

Integration complements synthesis because it's the process of finding a way to make seemingly contradictory ideas form some type of logical complementary picture. Here are some questions to consider:

1. Look at how the conclusions in the articles differ.

2. Consider how the situations which were examined or studied differed.
3. Consider whether the different conclusions could be related directly to the difference in circumstances.
4. Consider how you can use the different conclusions to create a framework that explains the occurrence of those variations or differences in the literature.

The result will be another part of the spider web, or framework, that allows you to accurately evaluate your topic and situation.

The critical thinking process required to develop a solid literature review is a constructivist process. Each literature analysis step builds on the previous, systematic step until a complete picture of the circumstance, question, or environment being examined is presented. Paramount to this process is ensuring your logic links are solid. Following the outline in this book and using the tools and questions to develop the information you present in your literature review will help you ensure those solid links are present in what can be an outstanding literature review.

APPENDIX A

Here you will find two forms you can use to assess your articles. The first helps with basic analysis of articles. It contains categories that may not always be useful to you depending on the type of article you're using. The second contains columns for evolution of each of the assessment types.

Article Assessment Form

This form (Figure A.1) can be copied and expanded. It is designed to give a basis for analyzing articles. In each column, as you read the articles place explanatory materials, as well as any noted issues with that category. Where no study is reported, examine the theoretical framework closely, and consider the studies and methodologies of papers cited in the article you are assessing.

Use it to catalog important information for use with your Article Analysis Form.

Literature Reviews Made Easy, pages 171–177
Copyright © 2010 by Information Age Publishing
All rights of reproduction in any form reserved.

Article name/ publication date	Question strong points	Question weak points	Framework strong points	Framework weak points	Methods strong points	Methods weak points	Analysis/ conclusion strong points	Analysis/ conclusion weak points

Figure A.1 Article Analysis form.

Article Analysis Form

Having completed the Article Assessment Form as you read each article, you're ready to use the Article Analysis Form (Figure A.2) to consider analytically each major characteristic of the article you've read. Please consider the strengths and weaknesses of each part of the article you've read. As you list the strengths and weaknesses in the form, be specific. What specific statement, method, or activity struck you as a noteworthy strength or weakness?

Both of these forms can be used as templates that "expand" as you enter information. For example, if you recreate the Article Analysis Form in Microsoft Word as a table with text it will automatically expand to make more room for your comments.

Question/topic addressed in article	Article title	Author	Study/article type (research, meta-analysis, etc.)	Theoretical framework of article	Questions/ hypotheses explored in article	Methodology used in article	Sample size used in study	Analysis of article and contents	Author's conclusions/ your conclusions

Figure A.2 Article Assessment form.

Critical Thinking Chart

This open table is designed to facilitate the development of comparisons and contrasts in the columns following the summary and analysis. Think of those columns as open for the evolution of ideas in a similar manner as that used to develop free writing and clustering ideas.

After you complete the entries on the Article Assessment Form for each article, examine your information and develop entries for the categories in the Critical Thinking Chart. As you'll notice, these are open columns designed to allow you to draw lines from different relevant article summary points to the column for the critical thinking type you've developed.

Table A.1 is a simple example and an expanded illustration appears in Table A.2.

As you can see, this becomes a living, breathing form to help you identify critical thinking points you present in your final literature review. Information involving an article doesn't have to be next to the article entry in the left column. You may also find yourself adding important facts from your Article Analysis Form as you add articles that have comparison or contrast points in relation to other, previously analyzed articles. As new literature becomes available, the articles you determine to be important may change. That choice is up to you. Remember, though, that the point is to present a saturation of ideas and perspectives so you're your reader has a clear picture of your knowledge on the topic (and, as a result of the knowledge available on the topic since you should have become thoroughly knowledgeable during this process). Finally, some of your entries about an article may not be listed in the same location as other entries if a point in a previously read article doesn't appear significant to you until you read another article with a point that makes it appear significant to you.

TABLE A.1   Completed Critical Thinking Chart

Article Identification and Important Point	Comparison	Contrast
Smith (2006) Tea in China most popular with young, upwardly mobile adults	Used by herbalists— (Jones, 2006) (Jacobs, 2006)	China tea popular for different reasons
Jones (2006) Tea from Spain most popular with herbalists developing tisanes Tea from China bitter and woody		Young adults— (Smith, 2006) Spain—natural medicine— (Jones, 2006)
Irving (2006) Tea from Spain rich and fruity taste		Different tastes of tea—woody, bitter— (Jones, 2006) Rich, fruity— (Irving, 2006)
Jacobs (2006) Tea in China popular with herbalists	Herbalists use teas to make tisanes in Spain and China— (Jacobs, 2006; Jones, 2006)	

TABLE A.2 Expanded Critical Thinking Chart

Article Identification and Important Point	Comparison	Contrast	Synthesis	Integration	Evaluation against U.S.-Grown Teas	Your Overall Conclusions
Smith—tea in China most popular with young, upwardly mobile adults	Used by herbalists—Jones, Jacobs	China tea popular for pleasure—Spain for medicinal purposes China tea popular with herbalists—Jacobs	Tea popular with both young, upwardly mobile adults and herbalists—Smith, Jones	Tea popular for different reasons—upwardly mobile—Smith; herbalists—Jacobs, Jones	Considerations to examine—whether tea in U.S. popular with both groups, and whether herbalists like certain kind	Still more information to gather at this point…
Jones—tea in Spain mostly popular with herbalists for tisanes	Jacobs—tea in China popular with herbalists	Young adults—Smith		Herbalists use teas (maybe widely, needs more research into how much) in Spain, China	Further consideration—are there other groups in the United States who like tea?	
Tea from China bitter; woody		Potentially Jones—bitter, woody taste for herbalists Question—young adults like woody taste? More research				
Irving—tea from Spain rich and fruity		Different tastes of tea—woody, bitter Jones; rich, fruity Irving		Rich, fruity teas and bitter; woody teas used for different reasons? (state possible, needs more research)	What is extent of Chinese tea and Spanish tea drinking in the U.S.?	
Jacobs—tea in China popular with herbalists	Jones—tea in Spain popular with herbalists					

CPSIA information can be obtained at www.ICGtesting.com
Printed in the USA
LVOW10*2232120314

377107LV00004B/90/P